P9-CJL-162

248.88
K584c

COURAGE
TO
CONQUER

America's Athletes

Speak Their Faith

Edited by
LeROY KING

WITHDRAWN

FLEMING H. REVELL COMPANY
WESTWOOD, NEW JERSEY

HIEBERT LIBRARY
PACIFIC COLLEGE - M. B. SEMINARY
FRESNO, CALIF. 93702
30511

The Scripture quotations marked RSV in this publication are from the *Revised Standard Version of the Bible*, copyrighted 1946 and 1952 by the Division of Christian Education, National Council of Churches, and used by permission.

COPYRIGHT © 1966 BY FLEMING H. REVELL COMPANY • ALL RIGHTS RESERVED • WESTWOOD, NEW JERSEY • LIBRARY OF CONGRESS CATALOG CARD NUMBER: 66-21798 • PRINTED IN THE UNITED STATES OF AMERICA • 1.1

DEDICATION

Branch Rickey was a man of indomitable courage. He exemplified the truths of which he spoke. While accepting membership in the Missouri Sports Hall of Fame at Columbia, Missouri, November 13, 1965, his last words spoken were these: "I'm going to tell you a story from the Bible about spiritual courage."

Mr. Rickey's words and spirit will live on in the hearts of men. It seems appropriate in these dedicatory pages to print some of his statements which characterize the magnitude and dynamics of his way of life. They also set the tone for this book:

"I'm not a theologian. I am a believer in God because I believe that Jesus was the son of God. I believe that we come to sense God through knowledge of the personality and the reality of Jesus. He was the truth. He said, 'I am the way; he who loses his life for my sake shall find it.'

"Jesus is not a myth. He's not a fraud. He is the light of the world. He died at thirty-three, a young man. At the very age when ball players with their knowledge and agility are at their best, this man died. What a marvelous thing it is for young manhood to have some sort of direction so early and so firmly hold this purpose in mind that they can say with great meaning, 'Don't you know that I am directed here, or there?' This is the secret, the explanation of a marvelously successful life—to have a worthy purpose for living and to be dedicated to that cause.

"Some sixty odd generations ago this man Jesus walked on the face of the earth meeting people, healing, teaching, and giving attention to any and all who called to Him.

"One of these was a little Jew. I don't think that he could see above the belt-buckles of the crowd. He was wealthy and a tax gatherer, unpopular, a clever tactician, and immaculately dressed. Everybody knew Zaccheus. I think that he had more moral guts than any other man in the Bible. When he heard that Jesus was in the vicinity, he boldly declared to his friends and family at the risk of unpopularity, loss of job, and ridicule:

3

DEDICATION

'I am going to get up before daylight tomorrow and I am going up to see who He is!'

"Whether in life or in death, it is the joy and purpose of these athletes and others to seek after this Jesus, to 'see who He is!'"

LeRoy King

INTRODUCTION

These words of the venerable Branch Rickey express so clearly the vibrant faith of a Christian.

He was unashamed of his faith and boldly declared the power of Christ in the sweaty, heated, competitive world of sports. He was one of the most versatile and powerful figures in athletics. His creative mind is responsible for many innovations in baseball, which have given maturity and integrity to the game.

More far-reaching than even baseball in the mind of Mr. Rickey is the influence of a movement known as the Fellowship of Christian Athletes, which he fostered for years as one of the founding fathers. He spoke of this organization with a burning passion and committed his time and energies to its cause of challenging young athletes and coaches to follow Christ in the fellowship of the church.

This book, the second to be published by the Fellowship of Christian Athletes, is dedicated to this man of great stature. It captures a few of the experiences, stories, and searchings of some of this nation's coaches and athletes. They speak from the heart of victory and defeat. They tell of their struggles and successes in finding faith's fulfillments.

I am proud and pleased to have a part in this book, and to work with the Fellowship in its cooperating ministry with the church. As a coach I know the meaning of victory and defeat. Being human we know we are going to fail sometimes. Along this highway of life there are temptations, mistakes, and sins, but if we remain acutely aware of this, we shall come closer to being the kind of person acceptable both to God and to our fellow man.

I have made many mistakes both as a coach and as a person trying to represent the one who was perfect, Jesus Christ. But my faith assures me that I am forgiven and empowered by God to correct my ways and defeat my adversaries.

These devotions are intended to reassure you of your part in God's scheme of things. They are written by men who have struggled through defeat, rejoiced in victory, and who continue in their pursuit of the Christ-like life, for they know that this is the only way that will bring everlasting victory in the hearts of men.

FRANK BROYLES

CONTRIBUTORS

LANCE ALWORTH

All-Pro flanker end with San Diego Chargers. Former All-American, football, University of Arkansas.

PAUL ANDERSON

Acclaimed "the world's strongest man." Has lifted 6,270 pounds. Won the gold medal in heavy weight-lifting class, 1956 Olympics. Currently Director, Paul Anderson Youth Home.

JIM BAKKEN

Outstanding kicking specialist, St. Louis Cardinals football. Second highest scorer in NFL during 1964 season.

BILL BRADLEY

All-American, basketball, Princeton University, for three consecutive seasons. Scored fifty-eight points in single game of NCAA tournament, 1965. Currently a Rhodes Scholar at Oxford.

JOHN BRIDGERS

Athletic director and head football coach, Baylor University. Also President of the Fellowship of Christian Athletes.

FRANK BROYLES

One of the nation's outstanding football coaches. Outstanding athlete at Georgia Tech; former head coach, Missouri University. Currently head football coach, Arkansas University. Voted "1964 Coach of the Year."

BILL CURRY

All-American, center football, Georgia Tech. Currently with Green Bay Packers.

RIP ENGLE

One of the nation's most successful football coaches, now retired. Former head football coach, Penn State University. Has also served as past president of the American Football Coaches' Association.

TOMMY EVANS

Three times national AAU wrestling champion, outstanding college wrestler two years, member of the Olympic teams of 1952 and 1956. Currently wrestling coach, Oklahoma University.

PRENTICE GAUTT

All-American football, Oklahoma University. Currently fullback for the NFL St. Louis Cardinals.

KEN HATFIELD

All-Southwest Conference, football, and All-American Academic Team 1964. Led nation in punt returns for two consecutive years. Currently a coach at U.S. Military Academy, West Point.

HARRY JACOBS

Outstanding middle linebacker, AFL championship, Buffalo Bills.

JAMES JEFFREY

All-Southwest Conference, football, Baylor University. Successful insurance businessman, Fort Worth, Texas. Currently Executive Director of the Fellowship of Christian Athletes.

JIM KAAT

All-Star and World Series pitching ace, Minnesota Twins.

FRANK McGUIRE

Successful basketball coach at St. John's University, University of North Carolina, and of the professional Philadelphia Warriors. Currently head basketball coach at the University of South Carolina.

PAUL NEUMANN

Outstanding basketball player and captain at Stanford University. Currently guard with San Francisco Warriors.

BOB PETTIT

All-American, basketball, Louisiana State University. All-time professional great, St. Louis Hawks. Currently in banking business, Baton Rouge, Louisiana.

BOB RICHARDS

Olympic Gold Medal Champion, pole-vault 1952 and 1956. National Decathlon champion. Currently Executive Director, Wheaties Sports Federation.

BOBBY RICHARDSON

All-Star second baseman, New York Yankees. Consistently outstanding defensive fielder, he also has been one of the leading hitters of the team.

CAZZIE RUSSELL

All-American, basketball, University of Michigan.

DON SHINNICK

Outstanding football fullback and guard at UCLA. Named "Outstanding Lineman" in 1956 East-West Shrine game. Currently linebacker for Baltimore Colts. Played on the 1958-1959 Championship Team.

STEVE SLOAN

All-American in high school and All-American, football, Alabama University. Broke every Alabama passing record, led team to victory, 1966 Orange Bowl classic. Voted "most valuable player" in this game.

BRIAN STERNBERG

World's record holder in pole-vault 1963. Currently Pacific Northwest area representative, Fellowship of Christian Athletes.

JERRY STOVALL

All-American, football, Louisiana State University. Currently outstanding defensive back with the St. Louis Cardinals.

BOB TIMBERLAKE

All-American quarterback, University of Michigan. Led team to 1965 Rose Bowl championship. Currently with New York Giants and student at Princeton Theological Seminary.

DOUG WEAVER

Outstanding linebacker, Michigan State University. Member of the 1952 national championship team. Assistant football coach at Michigan State University and University of Missouri. Currently head football coach at Kansas State University.

DAVE WICKERSHAM

Outstanding pitcher for the Detroit Tigers. Won nineteen games in the 1964 season.

JOHN WOODEN

All-American, basketball, Purdue University and one of the all-time greats. Head basketball coach at UCLA, his teams won two consecutive national championships. Only major college team in 1964 to go undefeated.

CONTENTS

I

"SEEKING"

A Meaning to Life

KEN HATFIELD

Knowing God

> . . . we had courage in our God to declare to you the gospel of God in the face of great opposition. For our appeal does not spring from error or uncleanness, . . . we speak, not to please men, but to please God who tests our hearts. . . . being affectionately desirous of you, we were ready to share with you not only the gospel of God but also our own selves, because you had become very dear to us (I Thessalonians 2:2-4,8, RSV).

IT'S GREAT to play on a winning team—and to be national champions! It's also exciting to be selected to the All-Southwest Conference team and the All-American Academic team, which I was in 1964. In all my twenty-two years I feel God has given me everything, but in return I have given Him very little.

I didn't used to feel this way. As a matter of fact, I was satisfied, going about my old ways, running around, and looking after myself. A typical attitude for those of many my age. But something happened to me in 1964 that changed both my thinking and the course of my life.

My football career came to a close in 1964, and the following summer I graduated from the University of Arkansas. I had always been active in athletics. While in high school I was fortunate to be selected for the all-state football and basketball teams, and as a member of the state championship American Legion baseball team. Although I weighed only 165, I wanted to continue to play football, so I enrolled at the University of Arkansas.

My coaches there taught me many things, especially

to be confident of my own abilities. I learned to improve in pass-defense and in returning punts. In my junior and senior years I led the nation in punt returns. Our Razorback team became co-champions of the Southwest Conference my junior year and national champions in 1964.

That summer I was invited to attend the Fellowship of Christian Athletes National Conference at Estes Park, Colorado. Coach Broyles encouraged me to attend. I decided to go, so I could meet some of the top athletes and also know more about this Christian movement. I also was told that I might be asked to talk about my faith in God.

On the flight to Denver I tried to determine when I came to know God. I started writing and before landing in Denver I had listed seventeen different times that I thought I had first come to know Him. At last I felt that I had enough material to talk about at the conference.

The first person I met at the Denver Airport was Bob Timberlake, All-American from Michigan, who is studying for the ministry and playing for the New York Giants. We joined others headed for the conference and started the seventy miles to Estes Park. I was new and alone. I wanted to get into the conversation, so I thought that I would bring up the subject of football in hopes of drawing some attention. But Bob started the conversation by asking what God meant to us in certain Bible passages. I was shocked! There I was thinking of me first, and Bob was thinking of God first. I knew then I was in for trouble.

At the conference I heard inspiring messages from such men as Coach Broyles and Bill Curry, All-American center from Georgia Tech, who spoke about putting God first in one's life. Their words and example reached me and for the first time in twenty-two years, I stopped to consider my life. I had been living for football, sports, and popularity. But most of all I had been putting my own interests first.

That week another person touched my life in a way more than he will ever know; that person was Coach Milo Lude of Colorado State University. He had asked me to speak on one of the afternoons of my faith in God. I told him I had tried to develop my thoughts, but after listening to some of the other speakers, I was uncertain about the validity of my faith and felt that I couldn't talk. I said that I had never heard "the thunder crash and lightning roar," nor any other visible sign of God's speaking to me.

His answer was: "I haven't heard God's voice in that way either." He went on to share with me his belief that the Christian life is a series of beginnings; that a Christian tries each day to do the best he can for God. Then he summed it up by saying: "The only sin God cannot forgive is the sin of giving up."

This was the first time I had really talked about all my problems. Back in Arkansas I was too proud to admit that I had problems. I learned here a most important fact: God is an everyday God, and not just a Sunday deity. Thanks to all the people at the conference, I learned that one could talk any time, any place, about God, or about any of one's problems.

I came back to my home in Helena, Arkansas, and in church I listened more carefully to my pastor. At the end of the service that first Sunday he gave the invitation to anyone who wanted to profess his belief in God to come forward. I hadn't planned to go to the altar that day, but as the final hymn was being sung my conscience seemed to say, "If you really believe what you told those people at Sunday school this morning, you will stand up and be counted for God." I moved up to the altar and to the pastor. I didn't know what to say, but the words came out: "I think I have found God." My parents and friends came down to the altar for prayer with me. I guess I consider that day the greatest one in my life, when I joined the greatest team of all—God's team.

I am not a complete Christian now, for to me there is only one true Christian—Jesus Christ. I make mistakes every day, but I try to improve. I keep trying. I talk with God now and ask Him to stay with me. I may lose some innings in the game, but we will win together.

I will not give up.

Prayer

I know it isn't easy to talk to others about You, dear God, but it can become more natural as I look to Thee constantly in prayer and devotion. I want my life to be the best witness to Your power and love and may the words of my mouth and the meditations of my heart be acceptable to You. Amen.

JIM BAKKEN

The Wisdom of Listening

> He whose ear heeds wholesome admonition will abide
> among the wise.
> He who ignores instruction despises himself, but he who
> heeds admonition gains understanding.
> The fear of the Lord is instruction in wisdom, and
> humility goes before honor (Proverbs 15:31-33, RSV).

I HAVE ALWAYS been active in athletics. I don't know
what I would have done as a youngster without some
sport. It was hard to pull me away from a playground or
a street football game. I thank my parents for allowing
me to participate in athletics. There was no question in
their minds that this is where I should be, if I wanted to
be. We always went to church and Sunday school on
Sundays.

I will never forget one experience that I had in our
Sunday school class. We visited another Sunday school
class which had Alan Ameche as a guest speaker. I wasn't
much over eight years old, but I will never forget that
moment as long as I live. He could have been the president of U. S. Steel, or some other prominent person, and
probably I wouldn't have remembered his name. But this
was my hero—a great football player!

Although I am crazy about baseball, too, football is my
profession. Maybe this was due to my high-school baseball coach in Madison, Wisconsin. He was a fine Christian
man whom I respected very much. I still see him as often

18

as I can. Although I felt the same way about my other coaches, I particularly looked up to him. I wanted to play baseball, but I went to college on a football scholarship, mainly because we had a good team in high school.

At college I had a fine first year and was elected captain of the freshman football team, so I thought that I was on my way to a good career in football and in baseball. In my sophomore year I played behind an All-American quarterback, Gale Hackbart, who led our team to the Big Ten championship. I split the time pretty much with him as a quarterback and had enough success to make the honorary All Big Ten team as a sophomore. I was even mentioned as a player of future stature. Then things started to happen.

It was my first experience away from home and here I was a young sophomore having ideas of real greatness, so I got a little cocky. Our football coach wanted me out for spring practice. I actually defied him and said, "No, I am going to play baseball this spring."

He said, "Well if you are going to be our quarterback next year, you have to be out for spring football." But I went ahead and played baseball. I know now that I suffered for this because other men out for spring practice gained ground from the practice. That fall as a junior I found myself scrambling for a job that I thought would be mine. An excellent player, Ron Miller, beat me and several others out of the job and became our quarterback for the next two years. So the job I thought was mine and a chance really to go in football seemed to be lost. I was relegated to the kicking duties and became the punter. I had place kicked before, too, but I had never punted much. So I started to work on these specialities. I started to work on it and felt that I was getting better, and also contributing to the team. I think I could credit our pastor for helping me the most. He still is the one I go to when I am in a dilemma and need spiritual counseling. My father died during this time that I was having my knocks in football. It was a great shock to us all, but I think that Dr. Weave, his messages on Sunday, and my personal contact with him set me back again on a straight line.

Following graduation, I had a chance to try out with the Los Angeles Rams. I went out to California as a rookie and thought I was pretty good. Again I didn't follow the routine that you should as a rookie by working hard at what you are doing, at being well-disciplined and conscientious, and at sticking to the rules. I got off the beam and suffered for it. I didn't perform well and was cut. When a rookie gets cut, nothing can be right. I mean everything seems to be going wrong. I was feeling bad and I was on my way home from Los Angeles.

On the way I called home and was told by my mother that the St. Louis Cardinals and the Green Bay Packers had both called and were interested in a kicker. I called Green Bay, of course, since it was close to my home. They told me that St. Louis had already picked up my waiver. So I called Wally Lemm, the coach, who told me to try to get to Omaha Friday night for practice. I drove straight through, and practiced with them that Friday night without any sleep. I am sure I was unimpressive. However, I did play the next night as a punter and this became the turning point in my career. I had never punted so poorly in my life; I think that I had a twenty-five yard average. My little girl can kick that far. But somewhere during the game in trying to tackle a receiver, I was kicked in the face. My nose was broken and I received lacerations around my eyes and nose which required a few stitches. I couldn't see out of one eye and had all kinds of headaches along with it. The next day I drove to St. Louis with Pat Fisher and another teammate and checked with the doctor, who fixed me up.

It's ironical how down I felt getting cut from Los

Angeles, then flubbing another chance with St. Louis. On top of that was my not knowing what would happen to me. But as I look back, my getting hurt was a blessing. The Cardinals kept me on because I was injured. They had no choice, so they kept me on for a period of thirty days, which is the minimum waiver of time that a player is to be kept in case of an injury.

During this time I really took stock of myself and started to work out again with the Cardinals, practicing my kicking earnestly. Also I worked at defensive back. As the season passed, I was put on the active roster and in the first game against Dallas somebody was hurt and I was able to play. I knocked down a couple of passes, so things seemed to be brightening.

At this same time I was making wedding plans. I had been going with my girl since about the third grade. We were married, my football career improved, and ever since then my outlook toward the church, my family, and everything has been different. It has been more secure and stable. I seemed to have direction now, whereas before I was just thinking of myself and what a big guy I could be.

I owe so much to so many people. Life has more meaning now. If I can make a favorable impression on some boy by the example of my life, I'll feel that I have accomplished something worthwhile.

Prayer

Help me, O God, to be strong enough to know when I am weak, and brave enough to face myself when I am afraid. Each moment of my life I will consciously be sensitive to Your touch and receptive to Your wisdom, following the example of Jesus. Amen.

TOMMY EVANS

God First

"You shall have no other gods before me.

"You shall not make for yourself a graven image, or any likeness of anything that is in heaven above, or that is in the earth beneath, or that is in the water under the earth; you shall not bow down to them or serve them; for I the Lord your God am a jealous God . . ." (Exodus 20:3-5, RSV).

I DID NOT realize it when I was in college, but I had another god I was worshiping more than our heavenly God. This god was wrestling. I came to realize this in my sophomore year at the University of Oklahoma. I was more dedicated to wrestling than to either God or to my education. Wrestling took first place in my life.

In my first two years at Oklahoma University I was the last one to leave the wrestling room. I would stay as long as there was someone to wrestle. On week-ends I would climb a wall under the stadium and break into the wrestling room, just to work out. I have worked out on Sunday when I know I should have been in Sunday school and church. The coach did not make us work out on Sundays. I did this on my own. The bad part is that all of this time I believed I was a good Christian just because I confessed to being one, and would go to church about seventy percent of the time. I also faithfully said a prayer before each of my matches. I got to the point where I was praying to win, not for help, or to do my best. I was win-

22

ning so I thought I had the right answer to my prayers.

My first varsity year, as a sophomore, I won fifteen straight matches, had six straight pins, won the Big Seven Championship, and was now wrestling for the National Championship. I was wrestling in the last period and was behind by two points. I started praying for God to help me win; but I lost the match. This was quite a letdown to me. Not so much losing the match, but I felt that God had let me down. The next six months or so I was really mixed up and my faith was at a life-time low. One day I picked up my Bible and came across a passage that completely changed my outlook as to the way I should live as a Christian. This passage is Matthew 6:33 "But seek first his kingdom and his righteousness, and all these things shall be yours as well."

So beginning my junior year this was the verse I tried to follow and stand on. In my junior and senior years I won every match. I became a national champion and Big Seven champion each year. I was voted the outstanding college wrestler both years. I went on to win the National AAU three times, the Pan American Championship, and a berth on the Olympic teams of 1952 and 1956. In the 1952 Olympics I won six straight matches and was wrestling in the finals for the championship. I was behind by two points, as I had been in the NCAA finals when a sophomore. I asked God for help but this time in a different spirit. I wanted to do His will, whether I won or lost. I lost the match, but I felt differently this time, because I knew God had not let me down. He was good enough to help me get this far. God has been good to me and I believe it is because I am trying to stand on God's promise. I know I have fallen short of these promises many times, but I pray that I will never stop trying.

God has not only met His promise to me in Matthew 6:33 as a sports competitor, but also as a coach and father. I have found unlimited power and courage to overcome the greatest of temptations and the most subtle enemy of all—success.

Prayer

May I seriously endeavor to do Your will each day, dear Father. Even in the midst of tough competition and under the pressures of so many things, I will put You first in my life. This is my prayer in the Master's name. Amen.

BILL CURRY

Learning to Love

> Behold, I stand at the door and knock; if any one hears
> my voice and opens the door, I will come in to him and
> eat with him, and he with me (Revelation 3:20, RSV).

IT TOOK ME a long while to understand the meaning of
the love my parents gave me as a boy. My main problem
was that I never learned to listen. Sometimes I heard it
expressed intellectually, but I had never accepted it with
my heart. I was too wrapped up in my pet interests—football and myself.

I remember studying in a history course about the various things that people worshiped all over the world. I
remember thinking how foolish man had been to worship
creatures like crocodiles or snakes. I began to look at
myself slowly but surely and at the things I had been
worshiping. What I discovered opened my eyes.

I saw that I had friends who worshiped popularity and
that I was guilty of this to a great degree. Other friends
worshiped things like automobiles. But probably the most
foolish of all, certainly the most startling, was to realize
that Bill Curry had placed first in his life a little piece of
pigskin that carried thirteen pounds of pressure per
square inch. This was my God. It's a glorious game and I
knew that by playing football I could draw attention and
glory to myself. I was all for me and no one else.

In this unreal world of self-centeredness I was missing
out on the greatest things in life. I had gone on like this

for years without realizing how I had substituted an easily replaceable object for the most precious possessions man has—his church and his faith. About this time my football career was beginning to dwindle off. I had gotten a scholarship to Georgia Tech by the grace of God, because coaches admit today they don't know why in the world they accepted me. I don't either, but I was there, and I was way down on the ladder. I had been told by one of our Christian coaches that I was as high as I would ever be—that I was lucky to be there, so not to worry about it.

I was beginning to get discouraged. My god was melting away; it was letting me down. It didn't have the power and means to help me when I needed it. It was slipping out of my grasp. I saw other young people running as though they were looking for an accident, or trying to find the next party for kicks. They seemed to be like me, looking for something to fill a void, unaware that only God can fill a human life adequately. The fallacy of my life was that I had been placing exterior things first in my life.

This same coach came to me about this time, for some unexplained reason, and asked if I would like to go to a Fellowship of Christian Athletes conference. I thought: "Coach, a Christian meeting is dull and preachy. If you want me to be a linebacker, I should learn to be tough." So I told him I didn't think I could make it.

"Well, that's a shame," he said, and clipped off about ten of the greatest athletes in the world who would be there. I told him I would reconsider, and then finally I decided to go. I went for the wrong reason. I wanted to rub shoulders with the great men and sure enough they were there. Coach Broyles was the first speaker. Also, I had an opportunity to meet men like Bob Pettit and Bill Krisher, men who have dedicated their lives to Christ. It was a thrill to meet them and I couldn't wait to hear what they had to say. Yet, when they began to speak, I was disappointed, because they weren't talking about football, basketball, or baseball—things that I thought were really important. They were talking about something that I had heard about in church but hadn't really allowed to penetrate my heart.

They talked about a personal relationship with God through Jesus Christ. I began to listen and to learn. I was doing some tall thinking for the first time in my life. I began to see that these men had qualities that I could not deny. I wanted them. I wanted to find out how to get them. While I was there, they told me. By believing in Christ, His teachings and His life, and accepting Him as personal Lord and Saviour, I could become a Christian. When this self-denial takes place and one thinks of others and his Lord first, life takes on reasons for being. Only by this step of faith did I find a satisfactory purpose for going out on the football field or the basketball court, or for being a coach. This is the same reason a man should decide to become a business man. The basic reason for living is to glorify God and not ourselves. One lives not that he may walk around with a holier-than-thou attitude, but that he may demonstrate an attitude of love—a love so amazing, so divine that others will be led to look at his life and say with enthusiasm, "That's for me."

Prayer

Dear God I know that it hurts sometimes to look at one's self critically, but it helps. Guide me to think of myself as a child of Yours and therefore to live as one. In the spirit of the Master. Amen.

FRANK BROYLES

Trusting

> "Therefore I tell you, do not be anxious about your life, what you shall eat or what you shall drink, nor about your body, what you shall put on. . . .your heavenly Father knows that you need them all. But seek first his kingdom and his righteousness, and all these things shall be yours as well.
>
> Therefore do not be anxious about tomorrow, for tomorrow will be anxious for itself. Let the day's own trouble be sufficient for the day (Matthew 6:25,32-34, RSV).

THERE ARE TWO young men walking along the pages of the New Testament who stand out in my mind. One of them was stoned to death by a mob. He was young, full of life, but even as he died, he was able to look steadfastly into the heavens and see the glory of God. As he breathed his last, he asked forgiveness for those who stoned him. He had the deep convictions of a Christian.

Also on these same pages is a rich young ruler who heard Jesus talk about a new kind of life. He was interested. So he went to Jesus and asked if he could join in this new life. When Christ told him what he'd have to do, that there were some things in his life he would have to give up, he walked away sorrowfully.

We need more of the courageous Stephens in every community. There are those who are willing and eager to stand strong by their convictions and face the crowd. These young men are the kind who continue each day seeking ways of becoming better Christians. I have been fortunate in having many of these young men on my teams, men such as Lance Alworth, Ken Hatfield, and dozens of others. They have made lasting impressions on the university and the entire state of Arkansas. Their spiritual depth added a new dimension to our teams.

One of these men I refer to is Jim Collier. He was a great conference end for the Razorbacks a few years ago. He had been there for three years but hadn't played much. As a sophomore he was red-shirted, which means he didn't play enough even to affect his eligibility.

When I put a list up on the bulletin board asking for boys who would like to go with me to the F.C.A. conference in Estes Park that summer, I was amazed that Jim Collier signed. I didn't think he cared. But he came and learned, absorbed, listened, and was most receptive. That fall he reported for football and it wasn't three days before he was on the first team. He made all-conference that year and this as a senior. After graduating, he signed to play professional football with the New York Giants. He played there three years and is now coaching at L.S.U. I know what can happen to a person if he is receptive, if he wants to be changed.

I'm grateful that as a teenager I had a family who took me to church. They always did. I've known nothing else but going to Sunday school and church. I want my children to have the same experience. I can remember as a teenager hearing someone say to me, "It's either all, or nothing; there's nothing halfway about being a Christian." I knew that I was a "halfway" Christian. I knew there were some things that I enjoyed doing that Christ might frown upon. So I would say to myself, "I'm just fifteen years old, or sixteen, or eighteen—I've got plenty of time to make Christ everything in my life. I've got plenty of time ahead. I'm just a teenager. I've got a whole life ahead of me."

That was a mistake. Someone tells the vivid story about

the Devil, who wanted to destroy man while on earth. He called in all his chief assistants and first turned to Anger. Anger stood up and he said, "Mr. Devil, I can go and destroy man. I will set brother against brother; I will get them so angry with one another that they will destroy each other." Then he turned to Lust, who said, "I will defile men's minds. I will make love disappear and men will turn into beasts." Then Greed said, "Allow me to go, Mr. Devil, and I will instill in men's hearts the most destructive of all passions—man's uncontrollable desires will destroy him." The twins, Gluttony and Drunkenness, told how they could destroy man. Envy, Jealousy, and Hate gave their versions. Then Idleness gave his pitch. But the Devil was not satisfied with any of these.

Finally his last assistant stood up and he said: "I shall talk to man persuasively in terms of all that God wants him to be. I shall tell him how fine his plans are—to be honest, clean, and bright—and I shall encourage him in all good purposes of life." When the Devil started to say something, the assistant said: "Just a minute, sir, I'm not through. I shall tell man that there is no hurry; he can do all of these things tomorrow. I shall advise him to wait until conditions become more favorable before he starts."

The Devil looked up with a smile and he said, "You are the one to go and destroy man." It was Procrastination.

I feel I'm one of the luckiest people in the world. I have a wonderful wife and six young, healthy children. I am in what I consider to be one of the finest professions in the world. I also think I have one of the greatest jobs in America. I have so many things for which I am extremely thankful. Who do I thank? I am indebted to friends, family, and others, of course. But I also know that everything I have, everything you and I possess is a gift from God. What you *have* is God's gift to you, and what you *are* is your gift to God.

You know, some people sometimes like to think of Christianity as being complicated. I'm not very learned in theology, but I know one thing—I have in my heart a child-like faith and a trust in Jesus Christ. Do you know what I mean by a child-like faith? Let me give you an illustration.

I was up in the mountains of Northern Arkansas one summer with my twin girls, who were six years old. We were going through this cave with our guide when all of a sudden he said, "Now we'll turn the lights out and you'll see the natural glow." As soon as my youngsters knew that it was going to be dark, both of the little girls came up to me and said, "Daddy, hold my hand." I looked down at them and knew here was an example of the trust God wants us to have. All they asked was to hold my hand. They didn't ask, "Dad, are we going to be safe? Are we going to get hurt? Is something going to happen to us? What have I got to do?" They just said, "Daddy, hold my hand."

As I looked down, I said, "Dear God, give me the strength to have this trust; this child-like trust that I can hold hands and walk down the street whether it be light or dark, and know that you will use me and take care of me."

Prayer

Loving Father, I pray that You will take me, make me, mold me, and use me to serve Your purposes on this earth. Thank You for letting me be a part of all that is going on. Just help me to do more for others. Amen.

DAVE WICKERSHAM

Forgetting the Past

> Not that I . . . am already perfect; but I press on to
> make it my own, because Christ Jesus has made me his
> own. . . . but one thing I do, forgetting what lies behind
> and straining forward to what lies ahead, I press on to-
> ward the goal for the prize of the upward call of God in
> Christ Jesus (Philippians 3:12-14, RSV).

ALL I EVER thought of as a little boy was playing baseball
in the major leagues. So when I made the Grand Forks,
North Dakota, team my first year in the minor leagues, I
knew the pressure was on. I had to make good in order
to keep advancing.

Naturally I was concerned about winning and losing
ball games. The night before I pitched, I couldn't sleep;
and if we lost, I couldn't sleep after the game. This happened to me more often than I like to recall since we
finished in seventh or eighth place. I was pitching every
fourth day, so you know I wasn't too successful. I was
losing a lot of sleep.

This went on for a spell until finally I decided to take
stock of my weaknesses. I realized that my faith had been
sadly neglected. I re-read the Bible with deeper understanding and honest inquiry. One passage in particular
seized my attention: "Forgetting those things which are
behind (which is the ball game just over) and reaching
forth unto those things which are before, I press on to
the mark for the prize of the high calling of God in Christ
Jesus" (KJV). This put things into a new light for me. I

knew that I shouldn't worry about the game. I should try
to do my best with the Lord. Then I read again Matthew
6:33, which I had been studying for some time in my devotions: ". . . seek first his kingdom and his righteousness, and all these things shall be yours as well." Here I
was seeking first this baseball, trying to get to the major
leagues. But this put me on the right level of thinking.
The next year when I had grown more in the Lord, I took
this attitude, which has remained my philosophy. "Let
the Lord's will be done in the game. Seek first His will
and not that of winning at all costs." I'm able to sleep at
nights both before and after games without worrying
needlessly.

I haven't always practiced regular devotional reading. I
actually started having daily devotionals when I was a
student at Taylor University in Upland, Indiana. I didn't
realize that a lot of people have such devotionals. I attended church on Sunday morning and evening as a boy,
and occasionally on Wednesday night. Although I had
accepted Christ as my personal Saviour when I was
twelve years old, there was no major transition in my life.
I just realized that my faith had only been one of an in-
tellectual acceptance.

Fellowship with other Christians has helped me to dig
a little bit harder in reading the Bible and making my life
more consistently Christian. As I speak to groups about
my faith, I find myself becoming more confident and enthusiastic about this wonderful way of life.

I know that other teams in the majors have players who
continue regular Bible study and discussions throughout
the season. The Minnesota Twins have as many as nine,
maybe more. An hour and fifteen minutes before the bus
leaves for the ball park on the road trips, this group meets
for prayer and devotionals. This doesn't guarantee victory,
but I know it has benefited many players personally.

My dad was another who instilled the spirit and desire

to play ball and to live as a Christian at the same time. He gave me the opportunity to play both baseball and basketball any time there was a practice, or any time kids could come to play.

The first ball game I ever pitched was at a Bible camp near my home when I was twelve. Jack Augustine, my minister's son, who was a couple of years older than I, started asking questions about Christ. This started me thinking along more serious lines. Reverend Augustine helped me along the way to relate the truths of the Christian life to my sports experiences. He is a fabulous Christian and dearly loved by everyone in the community. He showed me how to put my trust in God's care each day, trust which has carried over into my adult life.

My wife, Carol Sue, and I begin each day in prayer. We ask God to show us His will for the day and to give us the desire to seek Him. Naturally starting out the day like this gives you an interest in trying to stay in the center of His will all day. I know that. I am far from perfect, but when decisions come up, I usually have a way of knowing whether this is the Lord's will. I'm not saying that I have a direct pipeline to God, but I know that I feel confident in God's letting me know what is best in His strange, yet compelling ways.

I know that He helps me, even in ball games. I pray for the Lord's will to be done in each game—win or lose. I pray that He will help me to do my best, but sometimes my best seems to be getting knocked out of the box in the first inning. It has happened before.

In one particular game we played in 1965, I wanted to win so badly. This was the time. We were playing the Yankees, it was a coast-to-coast TV hookup, millions of fans would be watching, and I couldn't think of a better chance to witness and hopefully win the game. I was knocked out in the very first inning. The Yankees put the wood to me hard, scored four runs in the first inning, and went on to beat us about 15-1.

I was disappointed. I know I wouldn't be a true competitor if I hadn't had that reaction. But my attitude is different now—from what it used to be at Grand Forks. Now I might be disappointed for ten or fifteen minutes after a game, but before I get a block away from the stadium, I give thanks to God that I have Jesus. Athletics aren't the most important thing in life. What matters is what you do for Christ in and through sports, or in any other pursuit. Now when I lose, or pitch poorly, I can shake it off and prepare for the next game with a better attitude—God is giving me patience, strength, courage, and understanding to be a better athlete, a better father, husband, and friend. I pray that His will may be done through me every day.

Prayer

Dear Father, faith is such an important part of my life in athletics. But sometimes I neglect it in other areas of my life. Forgive me for my neglect and failures. Help me to increase my faith and love as You have shown me how through Christ our Lord. Amen.

JOHN WOODEN

Success

> Now as you excel in everything—in faith, in utterance, in knowledge, in all earnestness, and in your love for us— see that you excel in this gracious work also (2 Corinthians 8:7, RSV).

MY FATHER WAS one of the most remarkable persons I have ever known. He never had much in the way of material possessions, but he had a great deal more in other ways. We lived on a farm in Indiana, one mile from Centern, the biggest town I was ever in for a while. We had an elevator, a post office, and a country store. In those days you'd go in the store with a few cents and be able to buy more than you could carry.

Our little country grade school went up through the eighth grade. When I graduated, my dad gave me something which I have carried with me all these years. The gift was a piece of paper with this poem on one side: "Four things a man must learn to do, if he would make his life more true: To think without confusion clearly, to love his fellow men sincerely, to act from honest motives purely, to trust in God and heaven securely." This didn't mean as much to me at the time; years later I realized its real value and it has become an important part of my philosophy of life.

On the other side of this piece of paper is a creed. I have handled this so often I have practically worn it out. The creed goes like this: "Seven things you must do to be true to yourself: (1) to thine own self be true, and as the night follows day, thou canst not then be false to any man; (2) make each day your masterpiece; (3) live each day as it should be lived; don't put off until tomorrow what should be done today; (4) help others; a perfect life could be lived in helping others; (5) drink deeply from good books; one book alone would suffice, the Bible; (6) don't take friendship for granted. Study friendship, make friendship a fine art; (7) and perhaps most important of all, pray for guidance every day and divine guidance will come in some way." I've kept these rules, and they have been meaningful through the years in my teaching and coaching.

These words have enabled me to develop a better attitude toward victory and defeat, which every athlete and coach experiences. You can't judge truly the success of a team by the number of games it wins, as against the number of games it loses, because there are so many other things that enter into the picture. Likewise you can't judge the success of a person by his accomplishments. We do not have the same opportunities. Some will have more natural intelligence than others. Some will have better opportunities because of their environment. Some coaches will have better players than others. Some will be better coaches than others.

In the seventeen years I have coached at UCLA, I don't believe you will find a player who has ever heard me mention winning to him. We want to win as much as the next person. We play to win. Yet, I don't mention winning; I just imply it by what I teach. I tell our players that I'm not worried about the opposition; I'm worried about our boys. If each plays as he should, and at the close of the game he can honestly say to himself that he did his very best, the outcome of the game will be pleasing to him more than he realizes. I feel that perhaps my success as a basketball coach, or as a teacher, may be in direct proportion to my ability to get that idea across to my players and my students.

Now if they're going to be able to do that, however, there are some important things to practice, which I have learned from years of coaching and observing some of the best athletes of the nation: they must be industrious. If boys are going to do well, in their Christian life or in athletics, they are going to have to work. As has been told many times it's not easy to be a Christian. You have to work at it. There will be many temptations; there may be many disappointments, but practice and hard work are essential.

Also you must be enthusiastic about what you're doing if you're going to become a good Christian; you must be enthusiastic about your faith. You must be enthusiastic about your relationship with Jesus Christ. It won't be easy. But enthusiasm brushes off upon those with whom you're in contact.

I tell our basketball players that if they're going to accomplish the goals we set for the team, they're going to have to be in better condition than anyone else. This is achieved through hard work, but also by thorough mental, moral, and spiritual conditioning.

Our players know also that if they are going to become the best they're capable of becoming, they are going to have to have a knowledge of, and the ability to properly execute the fundamentals of the game of basketball. This is true for any sport. A brain surgeon must have more than a knowledge of brain surgery. He must be able to execute his skills and knowledge to the best of his ability, otherwise I would not want him performing surgery on my loved ones or on anyone else. It isn't enough just to have a knowledge of the fundamentals. You must be able to execute them. You learn to execute them by practice, hard work, and continued repetition.

We always stress the need for team spirit, a loyalty

and dependence upon one another. We learn a cardinal rule of life in athletics that the more you give the more you will receive. This means that each player must do his best so the entire team may benefit. He must be alert. He must be intent. He must have initiative and not be afraid to make decisions to get things done. The man who does nothing is the one who makes no mistakes. If he has initiative he is going to make mistakes, but he is probably going to accomplish things. An athlete must have self-control and a delicate adjustment between mind and body. He must have good judgment, poise, and an avid desire to compete.

All these qualities are essentials for success and the fortitude to excel. But there is no possible way to attain anything worthwhile without prayer and complete devotion to the one who gave everything for us that we might be the victors in life and over death itself.

Prayer

In life and in death, O Lord, be first in my life. Above all things let us first strive to please Thee in both joy and in sorrow, exultation and disappointment. Amen.

BOB TIMBERLAKE

Being a Christian

> Be watchful, stand firm in your faith, be courageous, be strong. Let all that you do be done in love (I Corinthians 16:13-14, RSV).

EVERY ATHLETE IS nervous and tense before a ballgame. You're excited about playing. There were some seventy thousand people watching, and an estimated seventy-six million people watching on television when we played in the Rose Bowl. So there's a reason to feel a sense of fear. During those few minutes before kickoff I feel like I have forgotten every bit of football that I know. It's in this kind of crisis before each game that I am able to sit on the bench, put my face in my hands, and ask God to send me the peace and courage that He has promised us through His Son, Jesus Christ. And every week He has done this. I knew that no matter what happened on that field, after some moments of prayer, nothing would separate me from the love of God. When you know this, you experience great freedom. You don't worry about a thing out on the football field; you just do your best confidently.

Well, this is an unusual experience for me because I was not always a Christian. By "Christian" I don't mean simply a person who goes to church regularly, maybe puts some money in the plate, and possibly teaches a Sunday school class. A Christian, in my opinion, is one who has a vital relationship with God through Jesus Christ.

I became a Christian in a strange fashion. In the summer of 1963 I worked as a night watchman in a Chevrolet plant in Warren, Michigan. I had a great deal of time to myself because half the night was spent walking between buildings and the other half sitting in an office building with nothing to do. Naturally there was plenty of time to meditate. One night I was thinking about a recent conversation with a fellow employee. I was appalled at my language. Every sentence had a "cuss" word in it. So I thought, "This is no way to talk, I'm going to change that right here; I'm never going to cuss again." So after about three days of working on it, I never did cuss again. I found that in subsequent weeks that more and more things came to mind about my personality which were wrong, which were detrimental to the athletic image that I think all athletes should project.

There were other things working on me—sermons I had heard in church, ideas of my friends, my conscience, and God. The other big thing at this time was the fact that a goal I had set for myself to be the most publicized quarterback in all time came to be so empty to me. I was searching for something which was more stable. I found this in the love of God.

I remember walking between the buildings one night and suddenly feeling everything about my life changing. I wasn't sure at first it was God; then I began to be afraid it was God. Perhaps this was the proverbial "call" to the ministry that we hear about and I wanted no part of it. I thought about this experience for weeks. Finally one night I said, "God, I can't stand it any longer; I'll do anything you want me to do." There was no lightning, no noises from the sky. I kept on walking and had a few tears, because I was so nervous and so upset. I think this was the start of my Christian conversion. I knew nothing about Jesus Christ at the time—about His sacrifice—about His leadership, about life. It seems phenomenal to me how God can work on persons in so many different ways. Since

41

I've been a Christian, I've had the question posed to me many times: "Can you be a Christian and a football player as well?" I know you can. There are three things that have helped me in being both.

The first is discipline. In football you've got to be disciplined: you can't smoke, drink, or run around all night and remain a good football player. The discipline for a Christian is a Christian life; we must spend time regularly in Bible reading, in prayer, in worship of God, and in service to our fellow man.

Second, we must do our best with what God has given us. I believe that God has given us all certain abilities. It may be in athletics or it may not be. I think He expects us to use our talents to His glory. There's a Bible verse that says, "Those to whom much is given, much is expected." Each of us here is given much and God expects much from us. I think it's our duty to find out what ability He has given us and how to use it for Him.

Third, we're called to work with one another. On our University of Michigan Rose Bowl team we had some athletes with black skin, and some with white skin. But they slept in the same rooms on road trips, ate at the same table, went to the same fraternity houses to eat sometimes; there was fellowship with one another. This is an example in football of working with one another. The fellowship is experienced to an even greater degree in the Christian life. You didn't see Christ shying away from anyone; He showed no favoritism. I believe we're called on to do the very same thing: to love everybody as Christ has loved us. This is His most precious commandment. There is no other way out. We must love one another as Christ loves us.

Prayer

Our loving Lord, I realize that any love I have for You is simply a reaction to the love that You have already shown me through the life of Christ and through His supreme sacrifice. Forgive me for my pride that gets in the way of my growth as a Christian. Help me to overcome my weaknesses and to become Your worthy servant by loving all mankind, including each person whom I meet this day. In the Master's spirit. Amen.

BOBBY RICHARDSON

The Gift of God

> For by grace you have been saved through faith; and
> this is not your own doing, it is the gift of God—not be-
> cause of works, lest any man should boast (Ephesians
> 2:8-9, RSV).

I HAVE HAD many thrills in baseball since I graduated
from high school and signed with the Yankee organization. But my greatest moments are always when I can
talk with young people across the country.

So many youth tell me they think of Jesus Christ as an
historical person. They know He died on the cross almost
2,000 years ago, but what they haven't done is to apply
His power and truth to their own lives.

Not too long ago big Bill Glass of the Cleveland Browns
and I spoke to the boys at a state penitentiary. As we
were walking through the halls, I recognized a young man
who was paying for his mistake with time taken out of
his life. I also remember walking out of the prison that
day and having the question of one young boy stabbing at
my heart: "Why is it that I hear Jesus Christ in here for
the very first time in my life?" We have only to read
in our newspapers, or to see on TV the opportunities of
witnessing and worshiping being taken out of so many of
our public gatherings across the country.

It reminds me of the story of a noted French jurist who
was an attorney for a murderer. In his address to the jury
he said: "Gentleman of the jury, my task is very easy. The

accused has confessed and a defense is impossible. But I want to say a few words. There on the wall I see a picture of the crucified Christ. We pay homage to Him. Yet, here is a man charged with murder who is here for the very first time in his life. It is you gentlemen whom I accuse; you that brag of your culture and education and are astonished when men reply with crime and vulgarity."

I remember about five years ago a few of us as athletes gathered in a certain section of the South to speak to community groups. Simply because we were billed as Christian athletes we were not allowed in several of the high schools. In many of our northern cities it is equally hard to get in if you are trying to tell about faith in Jesus Christ. It isn't always easy to witness to your faith, but I have discovered that it becomes more natural with each day's practice.

When I was fourteen years old, the pastor of our church took time to come around to our home and explain to me a verse of Scripture which has meant a great deal to me: "For God so loved the world that he gave his only Son, that whoever believes in him should not perish but have eternal life" (John 3:16, RSV). It was then I realized how God loved me enough to send His son to die for me personally. It was more than just knowing about Jesus; it was realizing His complete love for me. I can't stress enough the importance of having a real purpose in life— of knowing Christ personally and following Him.

This is the challenge I would like to throw to every young person. Examine your own heart and life, and honestly ask yourself these question: "What is my purpose in life; what is the meaning of my life?" There are three verses of Scripture which tell me of God's Word and purpose for our lives; perhaps these will help you. The first verse is Deuteronomy 10:12: ". . . what does the Lord your God require of you, but to fear the Lord your God, to walk in all his ways, to love him, to serve the

Lord your God with all your heart and with all your
soul. . . ." The second is in Micah 6:8: "He has showed
you, O man, what is good; and what does the Lord require
of you but to do justice, and to love kindness, and to walk
humbly with your God?" The third verse is from Mark
12:30: ". . . you shall love the Lord your God with all
your heart, and with all your soul, and with all your mind,
and with all your strength." These teachings have meant
a great deal to me and have given me direction and purpose for everything I do, including playing baseball.

In this world of professional baseball, football, or whatever the sport might be, there is always the chance of
being traded from one ball club to another. Sometimes a
professional athlete finds that he has to pull up his roots
and move quite often. This isn't easy to take because
there is always such uncertainty, anxiety, and restless-
ness. The story is told of a father who was happily
married, had a nice family, and was comfortably settled
in his home town. The children, of course had their play-
mates and liked school. The mother had her friends, too.
But then word came that he had been traded to another
ball club and would have to leave his home to report to
the other team immediately. The family was very disappointed, but he comforted them with this one statement: "I must go now, but I will prepare a place for you
and then bring you to be with me."

How fortunate we are today who know Jesus Christ
as our own Lord and Saviour, can trust Him and are
willing to faithfully follow in His footsteps. "Let not your
hearts be troubled; believe in God, believe also in me. In
my Father's house are many rooms; if it were not so, would
I have told you that I go to prepare a place for you?
And when I go and prepare a place for you I will come
again and will take you to myself, that where I am you
may be also" (John 14:1-3, rsv). It's a powerful challenge
and opportunity for each of us as athletes.

Teenagers—today are our leaders tomorrow. They will be taking over the responsible places in our churches, in our communities, in our industries, and in our nation. I am thankful that more and more young athletes and coaches are having opportunities to hear of Christ and to channel their lives in the direction of His life. This takes desire and courage. But if one has these qualities as an athlete, why not use them even more in living the life of faith and love set by the Master?

Prayer

Merciful God, help me to build my life so that my heart will be clear, my goal will be high, and that I will seek to master myself before I seek to lead others. In the way of the Master. Amen.

HARRY JACOBS

Influence

> If I then, your Lord and Teacher, have washed your feet, you also ought to wash one another's feet. For I have given you an example, that you also should do as I have done to you. Truly, truly, I say to you, a servant is not greater than his master; nor is he who is sent greater than he who sent him. If you know these things, blessed are you if you do them (John 13:14-17, RSV).

I HAVE been playing football ever since I was in the sixth grade. It has always been my favorite sport. My high school ball was played in Canton, Illinois. Other than a 7-2 record one season, we never had a winning season. I enrolled in Bradley University and anybody who has ever heard of Bradley knows that it's basically a basketball school, not a football school. In fact, I believe I received the last full scholarship that Bradley gave for football.

Our team surprised everyone—including our coach—my second year by finishing with a 7 to 2 victory! That was the best record we ever had during my years at Bradley, but not good enough for a championship.

After graduating from Bradley, I was lucky enough to be drafted by the Detroit Lions. They wanted me to play offensive guard. I weighed about 255 at the time and felt that I had the size and speed to make the grade. But I also was selected to play in the college all-star game. When I arrived at camp, the one coach there that I felt was the real factor to my being selected on the team was Lou Saban, the defensive coach. Lou wanted me to play defensive middle linebacker for him and since I felt that he was the one that got me there, I did. So I played middle linebacker, but a week went by at practice and the Detroit front office called the line coach to "get Jacobs out of defense and put him on the offensive line." They wanted to have me get some experience. At that time I was a bullheaded young man. I wanted to play defense, so I played middle linebacker. When I reported to the Detroit camp a few days later, I suited up for Sunday, but didn't play. The next Tuesday I was cut. I found out that you don't buck the system in pro-football; you do what they tell you.

I went from there to the Chicago Bears and made a play at the offensive guard position. I made it through the last exhibition game in 1960 with the Bears, but was cut again. I moved on to the Boston Patriots, where Lou Saban was coach, the man that I played middle line-backer for in that Chicago Tribune all-star game. I started as middle linebacker and played this position for three years. We had a good team but didn't always draw a large audience. I remember when we played the New York Titans on Saturday, the night before the Yankees played at home in a World Series game. Fans must have been baseball-minded because our crowd was so small it could fit in a telephone booth. Larry Grantham, defensive captain of the Titans quipped: "It's usually a custom to introduce the ball players to the crowd, but tonight I think we should introduce the fans to the players."

When Coach Saban moved to the Bufflalo Bills as coach, I asked to be traded to them, which was granted. I have been playing the last three years with the Buffalo Bills.

My first three years with Boston our team ended up in second place. My first year with the Buffalo Bills we tied for the Eastern Division Championship and the team that tied us was the team that I had just left, the Boston Patriots. We played them on the day after Christmas for the Eastern Division Championship. The field was covered with about an inch of ice, which made it better for ice skating than for football. The Boston Patriots proved to be better ice skaters than we were and beat us 26 to 8. So here again I find our team in second place and the team I had just left in first. Four years in a row I ended up in second place. But then came 1965.

Our ball club won the first nine consecutive games; then Boston beat us 36-28 in our tenth ball game. In San Diego the following week the writers wanted to know if the Buffalo Bills had the spirit to lose and come back. The game was a thriller! We played to a 24 to 24 tie, with three seconds to go. Pete Gogolack, our side-footed Hungarian-born rookie, kicked a seventeen-yard field goal and we beat them 27 to 24. We lost to Oakland, then won at Denver and came to the last ball game with an 11-2. We still didn't have our division cinched; we had to beat Boston. We would win the league if we beat Boston; if we lost, we would end up in second place again. So here in my fifth year of pro ball I find that I have been in second place four years—hungry for a championship— knowing that a victory will mean first place!

Our quarterback Jack Kemp took over and we beat them 24 to 14 for the Eastern Division Championship. We finally made it! I had my first taste of being on a championship team!

As much as this championship meant to me, being in the fellowship of young athletes at an F.C.A. national conference one week meant more to me than anything else. It was a revelation and an inspiration to sit and talk with these virile, bright young men—all interested in athletics, but more vitally concerned about what makes a person real . . . what values in life are the most important . . . how one can know God. I know that one of my purposeful missions as a professional athlete is to set a better example of being a Christian to the athletes of America. God will help me be that kind of person.

Prayer

I know, Father, that winning isn't everything and that this comes as a result of careful training, discipline, determination, and daily hard practice. Help me to apply these things to my life as a Christian as well as an athlete that I my share in the victories of life. Amen.

LANCE ALWORTH

Teamwork

> That which we have seen and heard we proclaim also to
> you, so that you may have fellowship with us; and our
> fellowship is with the Father and with his Son Jesus Christ
> (I John 1:3, RSV).

AS A PROFESSIONAL football player my primary job is to
catch a football. To do this proficiently I have to spend
at least thirty minutes a day doing nothing but learning
how to make the right moves and getting hold of that ball.
This takes plenty of concentration and self-confidence.

It doesn't take a person competing in a sport very long
to know the importance of believing in yourself, your
coach, and your teammates. Carrying this one step further,
I believe it's also fundamental that an athlete develop
strong religious convictions. I am grateful to my parents
for helping me in this respect.

Thanks to my mother and dad I guess I have always
been a professing Christian. I never really thought I was
an outstanding athlete, but my dad always seemed to
realize that I had a lot of natural ability and would encourage me to develop this ability to the utmost. He would
talk to me along the lines that "Christ gave this to you"
and that I should always dedicate my talents and efforts
in gratitude to Him.

He also instilled within me the idea that the more I
gave to God the stronger I would become. He would be the
first to remind me that though I might be reasonably suc-

cessful in athletics, someone will come along who is better. I have tried to live by that even now when I feel that I have had some measure of success. I stop and think that if somebody else had been in my shoes, he might have done a little better. This basic teaching as a boy has helped me to be aware of God's goodness to me and the debt of gratitude I owe to Him.

I have had many reasons to thank God for His help in professional athletics. I recall a game one year when I was caught in a pile up. As I tried to pull free, I looked up to see a tackler coming at full speed. I was caught in such a peculiar position I knew that if he hit me broad side my knees would be torn to pieces. Just before the impact I suddenly found myself free and I was able to move out of the hole. I didn't realize what had happened until later when talking to my defensive end on the side lines. He saw that I was going to be hit, so he gave a hard body block to one of the tacklers standing behind me, which knocked him off balance into two other men which freed me. He said "I thought you were in trouble," which was the understatement of the year. I thanked God that I wasn't injured and I also thanked Him for having such great teammates.

Before each game the players have a moment or two alone. In that time I ask that God will help me to use my ability to the very best and that our team will play together. There is such tremendous ability in our squad. We all have confidence that if we play to the best of our ability we will win. I have never really had any insurmountable problems as an athlete; most of my problems have been personal. I am human, just like everyone else, and we have had many temptations in professional sports. There really is no person who is perfect and not subject to such weaknesses as conforming to the crowd, enjoying some physical pleasures and other pursuits that would make you less than what you ought to be.

I know many people feel that a professional athlete has it made as far as success is concerned. But making money and having a big name is not my idea of success. I am grateful that I can make enough money to keep my family happy, but more than that I feel it is important that a person be happy doing what he thinks is pleasing to God. So many people seem to enjoy what they are doing, and, yet, they are not basically happy. Happiness to me is living the life that you feel is right conscientiously, and, at the same time, while doing this, enjoying your family and friends.

I know that it isn't always easy to stand up for what is right, particularly with a crowd looking on and someone teasing you. I used to get kidded a great deal when I first entered professional football; most of this was by older players who seemed to want to show off. As I look back now, I think how important it is for athletes to set the best example possible for their fellow teammates as well as for others.

As in football a person trying to live the Christian life must seek help from someone else. I have been fortunate in finding mutual strength and encouragement from some of my teammates, my wonderful pastor, who is so enthusiastic about his faith, understanding and beloved parents, and the most important thing to me, my family.

I am blessed in having a beautiful wife. Betty and I were high school sweethearts and we find it easy to sit down and talk things over. There really isn't anything that we can't tell each other. She is very out-going and an inspiring example to me, as well as a wonderful mother to our children. We do so many things together like fishing, picnicking, visiting the zoo, and playing outside. We do everything possible to share the joy of championship, mutual trust, and love which we have for each other. While I was playing at the University of Arkansas, Coach Frank

Broyles always was such a good influence on me as he is for anybody who plays under him.

I also experienced a real boost in my Christian faith and attitude when I attended the Fellowship of Christian Athletes conference at Estes Park, Colorado, in 1960. There were so many fine athletes and coaches there. The association with them has lasted in my memory and helped me to realize what a better example I must be to others. I don't know about others, but the companionship and help I receive from all these people makes me strive to be a better athlete and a better Christian.

Prayer

I am indebted to You, Father, for all the gifts of life so freely given. Help me not to take advantage of them but to use them wisely to glorify You and Your works. Amen.

II

"FINDING"

Power and Purpose

STEVE SLOAN

Conviction

> Jesus looked at them and said to them, "With men this is impossible, but with God all things are possible" (Matthew 19:26, RSV).

I WENT to Bradley County High School in Cleveland, Tennessee. To the best of my knowledge Bradley County High had never won a state championship in football. Its only claim to fame was having been slaughtered by our big rivals, Chattanooga State.

My sophomore year at Bradley, a boy named Farrell Fisher came in and organized the Fellowship of Christian Athletes. That year by coincidence, our football team won ten games. In the final poll we were nosed out of first place in the Tennessee point system 352 to 351.

When I was junior, I knew a boy named Billy Kelly, who was an inspiration to me because of his leadership and ability to overcome handicaps. Billy was president of the student body, president of the student council, member of the social league baseball team each spring, and coached a football team in the fall. He was quite a tremendous person.

All of this becomes more difficult to believe because both of his arms were cut off at the elbows, and both his legs at the knees. Billy stands about four feet high and walks on braces. When he goes to bed at night, he can take one leg all the way off. I wish you could see Billy hit infield to his little league baseball team. He can also shoot a basketball with remarkable accuracy. There's nothing that this boy can't do. And he always has a smile on his face. Billy Kelly helped me to realize that if any boy wants to be a good athlete, talent is great to have. But even greater is the need for desire, determination, and confidence. It's a matter of believing; even if you are the smallest fellow around. Knowing someone like Billy, Farrell Fisher, and others helped me to be a stronger person by the time I came into my senior year in high school.

Our goal, of course, was to win the state championship. We went through eight games undefeated. Our ninth game was with Battleground Academy in Nashville, Tennessee. We're not big city boys, and the idea of playing in that big stadium just about scared us all to death. But we played hard. In the third quarter we pulled ahead 20-14. They had the ball near the forty-yard line and were driving ahead. We had a little player by the name of Doc Davis, who suddenly called time out. Being the quarterback, I jumped him for calling time. He said, "I know what I am doing." He was a courageous rascal. He got everybody in a huddle, down on their knees, and right on the football field before some twenty-thousand fans, more than we had ever seen at one game, he led us in prayer. His prayer was that God might give us the strength to do our best; that God's will be done, always.

You can believe this or not—the next play Academy fumbled. We recovered the ball on the forty-yard line and I called an off-tackle play. I can't explain this to the girls because I can't even explain this to my own players; but all you do is fake to the full-back, hand it to the half-back, then run. We usually gain a yard on the play, but our left half-back went six yards for the touchdown. We finally won 34-14.

Naturally the team was happy and everyone was excited. When we got to the bus, our left end, Larry Link came up to me and said, "Steve, maybe some of these other boys who weren't playing don't know what we did out on the field. I think that we ought to have a prayer here on the bus to thank God for giving us the strength to win the football game." We told everyone on the bus to be quiet and then had a prayer thanking God for giving us the strength to do our best. This experience stands out in my mind as a true test of courage and determination.

This may seem strange to some; whenever I play football, I take Christ with me. He is my friend; I can take Him anywhere. He is a friend that will never disappoint me; He is loyal. And, man, when He gets hold of that weak spine that I have back there and holds me up in front of eighty-thousand people—by golly, I'm not afraid. I'm not scared because I know that with Christ I can always do the best that's possible.

Prayer

Most understanding God, help me to learn to laugh—yet never forget how to weep; to reach into the future, yet never forget the past. And among all the other things I pray for, help me to include enough sense of humor so that I may always be serious, yet never take myself too seriously. In Christ's name I pray. Amen.

PAUL NEUMANN

Surrender

> Trust in the Lord with all your heart, and do not rely on your own insight.
> In all your ways acknowledge him, and he will make straight your paths (Proverbs 3:5,6, RSV).

I AM THANKFUL that I have been raised in a Christian family. At an early age I came to know that the Bible should be my guidebook through life. It told me some specific things about myself—that I needed to know God as one who loves me; that I can always trust Him to empower me with strength and wisdom for the living of each day; and that whenever I sin by forgetting God and wrapping myself around my own selfish concerns, I become the loser. I die spiritually. The Bible also tells me that God loved the people of this world so much that He gave His only Son, Jesus Christ, for them to find inner peace, power through faith, and the means of having an eternal life of joy.

So I came to know this kind of God personally when I was ten years old. I know for sure that the Lord came into my heart because I felt it and I believed. I understood what is written in Revelations 3:20. "Behold, I stand at the door and knock; if any one hears my voice and opens the door, I will come in to him. . . ." I think that this is what happened to my life.

Then I also read that if one confesses Jesus Christ as Lord of his life and believes in his mind and heart that God raised him from the dead, he shall be saved. He shall have eternal life. It's as simple as that. There is nothing difficult about it.

The years went on and I went away to college to Stanford University, a great institution. But I got away from my Christian environment in college and my faith was readily tested. It was at college that I made some bad mistakes, took a few wrong steps, and doubted the Word of God. Certain professors, some guys that I hung around with, and kids in class created questions in my mind that I couldn't answer. I tried to reason these things out and the more I tried, the more confused I became. I tried to resolve my doubts separately from the Word of God. I even doubted the Word of God as being valid.

Then one thing followed another. I was disobedient to God and to my family training. I neglected my Bible reading. I neglected prayers. I neglected even to attend church services. I could always make excuses: "I had a term paper to do; I was too busy; I had a game to play the next day; I had to get enough sleep." It was easy to make excuses. Because of this, my witness suffered. I was a poor illustration of the Christ I professed to follow. I was not seeking Christ first; I was putting myself in front of everything else. I was more or less holding on to God with one hand and trying to gather everything else in my other. It just didn't work.

I heard a minister once say that the amount of time you are a Christian does not indicate how far you have traveled; it only indicates that you are on the right road. This was my case. I was a babe spiritually and I remained in the crib for many years. I really hadn't grown much spiritually.

Then through the help of a few friends, my family, and God's constant pursuing love, faith was restored. I realized that God requires a full surrender of our lives. This is the only way that one will have complete peace; but I discovered the thought that commitment of one's life to God must be a daily process.

There are many things I still don't fully understand. There are also many times I fail God miserably. But I'm learning more each day. I know that God wants me in everything I do. He wants me in my entertainment, my athletics, my studies, on a date—in all that I do. Whenever I keep my mind tuned to Him, I do better.

It's just like God is up in the press box and I'm on the field in touch with Him through my earphones. He is calling the plays to me. If I don't listen in, I get thrown for a loss—and ultimately defeated. But as long as I listen to the signals and follow God's guidance, I gain ground.

Prayer

Dear Father, I know that as long as I keep my eyes and thoughts on You, my faith will see me through; but when I look away from You, I become confused and frustrated. As with the early disciples, help me to look to the Master and draw from Him strength and confidence to live the right kind of life. Amen.

JERRY STOVALL

A Changed Life

> Have this mind among yourselves, which you have in
> Christ Jesus, who, though he was in the form of God, did
> not count equality with God a thing to be grasped, but
> emptied himself, taking the form of a servant, being born
> in the likeness of men. And being found in human form
> he humbled himself and became obedient unto death,
> even death on a cross (Philippians 2:5,8, RSV).

THERE ARE three men who have been very instrumental
in molding my life into what it is today.

The first one is a young man by the name of Prentice
Gautt. I met Prentice my first day of training with the St.
Louis Cardinals. He was one of the first men to greet me.
Being the first isn't unusual to Prentice. He was the first
Negro to enter the University of Oklahoma; the first Negro
to enter the University on an athletic scholarship; the first
Negro to make All-American in any sport. But Prentice
has another first for which I am very grateful. He was the
first man of any faith, of any race, to open the Bible and
his heart, and to talk with me in such an open fashion
about being a Christian.

The first day I was in camp, he talked to me of a certain
problem, which followed with the initiation of a Bible
study group. To my knowledge we were the only professional football team that had a Bible study group three
nights a week. Prentice was the narrator and the spokes-
man. Prentice Gautt. He helped me, a Southerner, to see
that a soul has no color.

The second man who has touched my life so deeply is a great coach, Paul Dietzel. I had the great pleasure of playing under him from 1958 to 1962, LSU won thirty-five games, lost six, and tied two. We played in four bowl games during that time. Coach Paul has meant more to me than any man alive except my dad.

Coach Dietzel gave me more through his coaching than I'll ever be able to repay. Even though he was a winning coach, he taught me one thing so important to my life— he taught me how to lose. Any boy can be a winner and easily accept victory. It's a wonderful experience to be runner-up for the Heisman trophy, to be All-American. It's gratifying to have your team-mates vote you the most valuable player. It's wonderful to achieve all of the great things that an athlete is capable of achieving. Anyone can accept these. But when you lose and certain groups begin to get down on you, it's a little bit hard to take. But Coach Dietzel taught me how to take defeat and come back even stronger, more determined to conquer. His Christian example has been an inspiration to me. With his help I have discovered that a man is tallest when he is on his knees in prayer, for then he walks with God.

The third man for whom I am everlastingly grateful is someone in my home town. This young man was one of nine children, five sons and four daughters. He was from a family that had not been known for its Christian living. In fact, it was the other way around; they were extreme alcoholics. Their morals were low. In fact, two of this man's brothers are dead today as a direct result of alcoholism. This man, and his brothers were noted for their drunken brawls, for taking advantage of every situation they possibly could.

This young man married at the age of twenty and started his family. But with a new family, he still avoided his paternal responsibilities. He continued to live the life of the past. He allowed no Christian influence in his home, even fought it. It's amazing to listen to the accounts of his children, and he has five. They talk of lying awake at night hearing their mother and father fight and curse one another—each one telling the other to get out and never to come back.

As these children lay there, tears streaming down their faces, the last thing they remembered was crying themselves to sleep. No one came to tuck them in; nobody said a prayer with them. And they always awakened in the morning with a start, wondering if their mother or father would still be there? It was never home; just a house.

An amazing change came over this man. During this period of struggle, several people in this small community knew he needed help. They counseled with him, and prayed for him and his family. Some eight years ago, this man became a Christian. About six years ago, he was made a deacon in his church. I wish that I could say he is one of the most shining examples of Christianity that I know. He is not. I know him quite well, too. He had five daughters, one son. I am that son. But I know this, as a Christian parent my dad gave me the greatest gift that a parent can give to his child, love.

I thank God for my father and for the life he is living.

I've often thought that it would be a wonderful thing to die and go to heaven to be with Jesus Christ. But you see, Jesus took care of that for me here. I don't have to die to have heaven. Jesus Christ has sent a little bit of heaven to be with me in my wife, my child, and my many Christian athlete friends throughout the world. I realize they are all human, too, but they help me to look through to the man they represent—Jesus Christ.

Prayer

Gracious God, I realize that I have so many responsibilities as an athlete and I need Your guidance to live up to them. And I strive to be worthy of all who have added to my life that I may contribute something worthwhile in the lives of others. Help me to truly follow in the footsteps of the Master. Amen.

CAZZIE RUSSELL

Power Through the Word

> With my whole heart I seek thee; let me not wander from thy commandments!
>
> I have laid up thy word in my heart, that I might not sin against thee.
>
> I will meditate on thy precepts, and fix my eyes on thy ways.
>
> I will delight in thy statutes; I will not forget thy word (Psalms 119:10-11,15-16, rsv).

SPORTS WRITERS have asked me many times, "Why do you believe in God and in reading the Bible?" This has been a big question to me over the years and I have given a great deal of thought to it. I don't know how it is with others, but reading the Bible regularly and praying keeps me in spiritual condition. This is as important to me as staying in top physical condition in and out of season.

I suppose the Bible always has meant a great deal to me because of my home training. My mother taught me the meaning of the Christian life in our home. Then when she explained many of the things about the Bible, this kind of put the frosting on the cake. I have been reading the Bible since I was a small boy. This conditioning has carried with me throughout my athletic career and has been an important part of my life. For one thing I know that prayer and devotional reading help me stand the pressures of ball games and school work.

I like to remember special Bible verses which have been built into my whole attitude of thinking about life.

One of my favorite passages is from Hebrews 11:1: "Now faith is the assurance of things hoped for, the conviction of things not seen." This says to me to have faith in God and self and to go out and do your very best, knowing that you will receive the blessings of God when you seek to do His will.

I also like the verse from Psalms 27:1: "The Lord is my light and my salvation; whom shall I fear? The Lord is the stronghold of my life; of whom shall I be afraid?" Another passage that speaks such a truth to me is from first Samuel 16:7: ". . . for the Lord sees not as man sees; man looks on the outward appearance, but the Lord looks on the heart."

I also learned a great deal about the meaning of the Bible from my minister, Pastor Clay, who was such an influence on my becoming a Christian. He talked to me about different passages of the Bible that would help in keeping my faith and gave me this motto: "Every saved soul is saved to help save souls." I have always tried to follow this motto.

I know that my faith in God and my understanding of the Bible have helped me in athletics. For example, I can look back on my sports life and not be ashamed of what I have done. I am proud that I have established a fairly decent reputation. Knowing that you have a certain influence on others makes you feel more responsible in setting the best example possible. I have always felt that it is difficult to lead two lives if you are trying to please God and be true to your faith.

I can think of a number of instances where my faith has helped me to keep my composure in the face of some great pressures. In some high-school games the opposition would try ways to make me lose my poise by actions such as pushing, hollering, and throwing insults. I remember in one particular game a boy from the South Shore stuck his finger in my eye, tripped me, and knicked my shins trying to stop me. It was all I could do to ignore him instead of retaliating. But I controlled my temper and simply worked even harder to play the best game I could. As a result we won and I felt stronger having kept my head.

There are many ways I believe a Christian can witness to his faith. I try to speak as many times and in as many places as I can during the off season, because it helps me to better articulate the meaning of my faith and to share my thoughts with others. I also think that you witness by the way you play. I am sure that some players have noticed that I pray by myself before a game. Before every game I try to liven up our team, which helps to ease the tension and keeps me a bit more relaxed. Once I hit the floor the tension is off and I know the Lord is helping me. Although I weigh 215 as a guard, which is heavier than most players in my position, I don't feel as weary.

I didn't get into basketball until I was in the eighth grade, and I really didn't start playing basketball until I was in high school. My physical education instructor interested me and had me come out for the team. Until then I was more intent on being a baseball player and dreamed of actually playing in the major leagues. My dad liked the Dodgers and I suppose my greatest heroes were Stan Musial and Willie Mays.

Once I started playing basketball, I really became enthusiastic. Also I was growing a great deal and stood about six feet tall. I started practicing jump shots, lay ups, and free throws. A number of us would go around the block to pick up a team and then play on the outdoor courts of the recreation centers in the Chicago Park District.

Our high school teams did fairly well and went to the state finals twice. One of the closest games we had was against Decatur, a game which we lost 49-48. In that game I scored twenty-seven points.

I enrolled at the University of Michigan and have been

fortunate to play on some great teams there. When I arrived on the campus, I wondered how many other students and athletes were Christians. I kept my eyes and ears open and soon found there were other fellows who thought a great deal about their faith and applied it to their athletics. I joined them with enthusiasm. These were fellows like Bob Timberlake, Dave Butler, John Clauson, Van Tillson, and many others. Also we were greatly assisted by the advisor of the Fellowship of Christian Athletes, Dr. Ernest Campbell. I will give Bob Timberlake most of the credit for helping FCA get started at the University of Michigan and for asking me to help them out. I have seen how God has worked through this group to help athletes study and understand more of the books of the Bible. We openly discuss our problems and seek solutions which are found through the Christian life.

One of the problems we meet in athletics is the use of profanity by so many players. We have talked about dealing with this. We try to get across to these athletes that it isn't necessary to talk this way, but we do it in a way to avoid any feeling of being "Holier-than-thou." I just ask such players if they couldn't find another word in their vocabulary, that what they are saying doesn't sound very good. Sometimes they'll oblige; but at least they'll respect your position.

We get into some good discussions. Some fellows don't believe because they are confused. I don't argue with others; I think that we accomplish more just by discussing and trying to set the best example by what we believe. I thank God for making Christ real to me so that I can become a better person and a better athlete.

71

Prayer

Father, help me through daily study of Your word to better understand the meaning of life. Strengthen my will to make my devotional reading better disciplined and more purposeful. Help me to share every problem and concern, each happy experience with You. As the Master would pray. Amen.

PAUL ANDERSON

The Strength of Meekness

> Above all hold unfailing your love for one another, since
> love covers a multitude of sins. Practice hospitality un-
> grudgingly to one another. As each has received a gift,
> employ it for one another, as good stewards of God's
> varied grace: whoever speaks, as one who utters oracles
> of God; whoever renders service, as one who renders it
> by the strength which God supplies; in order that in
> everything God may be glorified through Jesus Christ. To
> him belong glory and dominion for ever and ever (I Peter
> 4:8-11, RSV).

I HAVE BEEN asked many times, "What is your greatest
thrill in sports?" That's not easy to answer for I've been
blessed with many exciting moments in my athletic
career. One of these occurred an early morning on November 24, 1956 at Melbourne, Australia. At 2:00 A.M. I
had just completed the last lift in the Olympic games,
winning the gold medal! This was indeed a thrill! After
a minute of rest I was beckoned to come forward, to
climb the steps to the center pedestal. A sign was at-
tached on the first-place dais "U.S.A." Others gathered
around me; I could see the other lifters who had par-
ticipated from Iran, where weight-lifting is a national
sport; from Italy, South America, Europe, Argentina, and
Russia. As the thousands of fans stood, our flag was slowly
raised, the national anthem, *The Star-Spangled Banner*
never sounded better. That was an experience that would
bring tears to the eyes of the most complacent person.

But that was not the greatest thrill in my life. The one most meaningful to me was when I let Jesus Christ take over my life. Every minute of the day I continue to receive that same thrill, the excitement of serving Him.

I have discovered that it takes a strong person to follow Christ. His way isn't for sissies or the timid. You have to be strong because you will need to be an individual, you will need to give of yourself; there's no selfishness. As a Christian you help everyone you can. In everything you do, you try to reflect Him. As an athlete you reflect Him through your natural ability as a leader. This requires disciplined strength to *love,* to *serve,* to *do* your part in making the world a better place for everyone.

But there are those in every community who will make fun of you for being a Christian. They are really the weaklings. The weak really don't have Christ in their hearts; they are selfish, they're always going to join the gang, they're going to try to impress others, and they won't care how they do it.

Our country is full of followers, like sheep following one right after the other. We see article after article on the decline of the individual. So many times someone gets into trouble just trying to impress a group, trying to be accepted.

I can think of someone I know who appears to be tough on the surface. He goes around spinning the wheels on his car and you can hear him for four city blocks! He gets behind the wheel and goes out to sip a little suds! Now, man, he is tough! He thinks he's tough. A lot of them play sports. Many of them don't because maybe they've got a new car and they like to ride around too much. He seems to be tough; he's always being pointed out so you think you'd like to go around with him and be a part of his world. Just a word of warning. He might not be as tough as you think, if the situation would arise that would test him.

The worse case exemplifying this attitude I've ever seen existed in a little school down in Georgia. They have a club in the school of professing "atheists"; they say they don't believe in God. Well, I talked with them, must have been fifty or seventy-five minutes, and we argued awhile. I tried to give them some valid reasons for believing. Of course, they would come out with all these crazy questions and I would even go scientific and give them reasons why there must be a God. I even told them that there was a movement in the Soviet Union not long ago by some of the great scientists, who asked the Kremlin to recognize a Higher Power because they had come to the point where they admitted things they could never explain. This didn't seem to affect them. They asked, "Well, how do you know there is a God?"

I said, "I talked to Him a few minutes ago; that's how I know." I don't know if my words had any lasting effect on those young people, but let me tell you of a pathetic situation.

I wanted to know who started the group. I found out. He wasn't a delinquent; he was a young man from one of the finest homes in town. He was a good church worker—even sang in the choir. He was a gentleman in every way. But he had a situation at home that was pretty bad. He had an older brother who was held up as being *perfect*. Every time that this young man I speak of would do anything—would bring a good report card home—his parents would look at it and say, "That's nice, but you know what your brother did; you know what you've got to live up to." That had been going on all his life.

One night he was going to choir practice and was a little late. His parents were bugging him about it. They said, "Come on, let's go now; let's hurry up."

He was frustrated and finally blurted out: "Oh, I'm not going to go—I don't believe in God!" Well, his mother and daddy jumped off the floor and made all sorts of strange noises. That was what he'd been looking for, he finally got some attention all his own, for the first time in his life.

So the next day he rushed off to school to carry on the same way. Some of his fellow students looked at him out of the corners of their eyes, but a lot of them joined him. He was a leader and they went along with him. If he said there was no God, they were stupid enough to follow along. And he *was* getting attention. The pathetic thing is that all of these fine young men and young women were being led by one emotionally disturbed boy.

The person who thinks for himself and who thinks of others is stronger, wiser, happier than is the one who thinks of nothing but personal pleasure.

In Detroit they make fine new automobiles to be treated in a certain way. They are designed to be taken care of and to be driven on good roads. Your car will last longer when treated properly. That's the way the master mechanic and engineer designed it.

But if some idiot gets in it and takes off down through the woods having a big time, he's going to tear it up. This is also true of our souls and our bodies. They must be treated in the way in which they have been designed—as creations of God.

Prayer

Father, help me to be the kind of person who will stand proud and unbending in all of his defeat, yet humble and gentle in victory. Give me humility so that I may always remember the simplicity of true greatness, the open mind of true wisdom, and the meekness of true strength in love and thanks to Thee, I pray. Amen.

BOB PETTIT

Set the Standards High

> I can do all things in him who strengthens me (Philippians 4:13, RSV).

As I LOOK BACK over my career of eleven years in professional basketball, I'm proud of the record I've accomplished. I have set standards for myself in basketball, as I have set standards for myself in life. I retired in 1965 after eleven years because I knew I was getting older and would find it more difficult to meet these standards. I would be the most miserable human in the world if I returned and played below the standards I set for myself. As I look back over my career it's unbelievable that I had the highest score in the history of professional basketball. Talk about humble beginnings, I think I had the most humble of all.

I first went out for basketball as a freshman in high school. I played all year and usually got in the games just as the gun went off. When we were twenty points ahead, or twenty behind, the coach would send me in. I'd sit in the locker room after games and listen to the fellows who scored two points, or four points, and I wouldn't say a word. This went on all year because I never scored a point as a freshman in high school. This was pretty discouraging.

I went back and tried to play my sophomore year but was cut from the team. I made up my mind that basketball was what I wanted to play, so I started practicing.

I practiced three hours a day my sophomore year and continued this schedule until my senior year in college. Needless to say, my driving ambition was to be a basketball player.

In college, playing basketball was my main interest. I was so wrapped up in this and other interests that I drifted away from the church. I had grown up in St. James Episcopal Church at Baton Rouge, Louisiana. I attended Sunday school, sang in the choir—which set the choir back a few years—ushered, did everything. I let other interests crowd out my church life in college. But as I went into professional basketball, I wanted something more out of life. I was searching for some answers to some very important things. I seemed to be drifting in a vacuum.

I had an offer to go to Dallas, Texas, and speak in one of the Sunday services at a church. From that church I was asked to attend my first Fellowship of Christian Athletes conference at Estes Park, Colorado. That was the beginning of certain things that I'd been looking for.

I returned from this first conference and began reading more, speaking some, and thinking more seriously of ideas shared by so many of the coaches and athletes at the conference. Whole new horizons opened for me. I think I started to grow more spiritually. I began to talk to church groups and to others about my faith.

As I started to do this, an amazing thing happened. As I shared my ideas and thoughts with others and tried to help them, I found that I was the one benefiting the most. It's like basketball. Whenever I would set a pick for one of our guards, a switch would occur; and as I rolled to the basket, he'd bounce the ball to me for a lay-up. As I went to help someone else, I was the one that actually benefited the most. My intentions were not for my glory, but to help my fellowman.

I've come to believe that there are two responsibilities of paramount importance in every person's life:

1. The responsibility of a person to his fellowman.
2. The responsibility of a person to his God.

An athlete is one who has to lead. He has certain responsibilities to the people that look to him for guidance and for leadership. Everyone has this responsibility—with no exception—to be the type of person that others may look up to and want to model their lives after. You may lead a person the right way or you may mislead him by your example.

Last year I think I had the most inspiring thing happen to me. I was sitting in back of the auditorium at an F.C.A. conference listening to a young man I respected so highly. I had been with him at Lake Geneva, Wisconsin a few years before. He was probably the greatest basketball player in the country in 1965 and he is, of course, Bill Bradley.

He told the audience how he had been searching in his life, and hadn't been able to answer certain questions. He was at a very low point, when he picked up an album of our F.C.A. talks and heard my message. Listening to the things I had to say made a great change in his life. I guess one doesn't fully realize the responsibilities he has in just being an athlete. There are always many opportunities to help others every day.

There is a responsibility we all have to God, too. As I first walk into my church, I have a little prayer in which I talk to God personally. It's not a part of the regular service. But I share my time with God. Every time I do this it means so much to me because it's my opportunity to thank God for the many blessings I have received. He helped me to make important decisions two or three years ago which I'm proud to say I have fulfilled to the best of my ability. I was going to attend church every Sunday the coming year. I wasn't going to miss a Sunday! The only time that I missed during that whole year was during basketball season when we had to travel on a Sunday, and I wasn't able to get to a service. It did wonders for me to take time every Sunday to worship with others. Sometimes during the week I would walk into a church and just sit down in silence, meditating. I would ask God to guide me as I went through the days ahead. This discipline has made me so much stronger, just a simple thing like going to church every Sunday.

I think this will best explain the way I feel about my relationship with God. I know that no matter what happens, God will take care of me. If I stumble and I fall, do things that I'm not supposed to, get into trouble and need help, He is always there to pick me up. He is stronger and wiser than any person. I feel that God helps me to get back on the right path when I wander. It's the greatest feeling in the world to know that you have someone to help you whenever you fall down and get into trouble. That's exactly how I feel about my God.

Ever since high school I have been part of a ball club. Now that I have retired from professional basketball, for the first time I'm no longer going to be part of a basketball team. But I like to feel that I'm going to be a part of a much greater team; a team that's playing for much bigger stakes, whose ultimate victory means so much more than a basketball game could ever mean. I like to feel that I'm a part of Christ's team. I like to feel that even though I'm not the greatest player in the world, I am part of His team. I may just be a substitute, but I guarantee you I'm there on the squad. And one of those days when His team has to stand up and be counted, my name will be there.

It does me a great amount of good to be able to stand up in front of a group and tell them I'm proud to be a Christian. I'm proud that I go to church; I'm proud that I'm not a follower; I'm proud that I'm able to stand up and share some of the thoughts that I feel deep inside, some of the things that have meant so much in my life.

I'm proud to be able to say that I have accepted Christ as my Saviour and that He has given me something to base my whole life upon. For after all, we are not so much searching for individual gain or glory as for the victory of Christ in the hearts of men.

Prayer

God, we are constantly looking for answers to our problems, but so often looking in the wrong direction. Help us that we may constantly look to thee for our help and inspiration. May the glory I seek in athletics be directed to You, and not to myself. Through my efforts may You come to be known and loved by more men every day. Amen.

RIP ENGLE

Example

> Bear one another's burdens, and so fulfil the law of Christ. For if any one thinks he is something, when he is nothing, he deceives himself. But let each one test his own work, and then his reason to boast will be in himself alone and not in his neighbor. For each man will have to bear his own load.
>
> Let him who is taught the word share all good things with him who teaches (Galatians 6:2-6, RSV).

I BELIEVE that Christian athletes are in a better position to face the world and do the greatest good for mankind than that of any other group.

America is a hero-worshiping nation. Our people are going to worship somebody whether he be an exciting entertainer, a popular politician, or a great athlete. I've observed in my thirty-five years of coaching young men in football how each player is held in awe and admiration by youngsters everywhere who are crazy about sports and who may aspire to play on some university team.

I tell my players to be thankful for the privilege of competing. There are thousands of boys in the world who do not have that opportunity. Each season our boys are asked to take an inventory of their deeds, evaluating what has been beneficial to others and what has been abusive. In taking stock of themselves they usually come out counting their blessings, determined to try even harder to improve their personal lives and their skills on the field.

It isn't easy to improve one's way of living. With some

of us there are too many things which need changing. But I notice time after time that the boy who struggles to become a better person invariably becomes a better athlete.

There are a few lessons I have learned over the years which have helped me to face adversities and many temptations. These have become a necessary part of my life and my coaching.

I believe an athlete should exert leadership not through power, or force, but by example through enthusiasm, kindness, loyalty, cooperation, and performance. These are the qualities that count. Most of the world's ills come from leadership through force as demonstrated by the Hitlers, the Castros, and so many more.

The chairman of the board of a well-known national company wrote this challenging statement to his company. "You can command a man's time; you can command a man's physical presence at a given place; you can even command a measure of skilled muscular motions for an hour or a day, but you cannot command enthusiasm; you cannot command initiative; you cannot command loyalty; you cannot command the devotions of hearts, minds, and souls; you have to earn these things!" How well a coach realizes this.

A person will serve his Maker best if he accepts victory and great accomplishments with grace and humility. People will know a truly great athlete; they won't have to be told. I have always found that the fellow who does throw his weight around is never quite as good on that five-yard line. I recently heard a clergyman from New England say: "Talent is God-given; be grateful. Fame is man-given; be thankful. Conceit is self-given; be careful."

I believe that to best serve your Maker, you should live a religious life. This may mean something different to each person, but I think one of the things it means is to give your body as much cooperation as you can. Do not destroy the body that God has given you. Drinking and other excesses destroy body and personality. I have never drunk nor smoked in my life. This is perhaps nothing particularly great, because I have never given up anything of this sort. But I do know it is important to honor the body God gave, and to respect the body of every other person. Being religious requires self-discipline, some sacrifices, some enduring hardships and some service, all of which any of us can give.

If you would serve your world best and your maker, I believe that however discouraged, or disappointed, filled with despair, or depressed you may get, you should never lose your love of competition and your desire to win. Regardless of the odds, the conditions of the field, the hopelessness of the situation, you should never lose that value of just trying to win. You are going to lose some contests, most of them in fact, and you are going to win some. That's what makes it all worth while. If you lose a game, it still isn't all lost because if you have done your best, you will come out a better son, a better citizen, and a better human being. Confucius was a great philosopher and seemed to recognize some of the values in losing by writing this: "Man's greatest weakness consists not in failing, but in not rising every time he fails." I think that we have been in over 300 games and I know of five or six of these that we weren't given a chance to win, but we did. If you have had that experience in a game, or in life, you enjoy the great feeling of pride, exultation, and happiness that comes from winning. But also, above all, you enjoy the sense of satisfaction and gratitude.

The Christian way of life gives power and initiative to help a person steer his life in a proper direction. Without a compass or rudder a ship is not worth much; it isn't going to get anywhere. An athlete without proper guidance and motivation won't amount to much. But with the right attitude, plenty of confidence, and the right kind of steering, he will be able to give the leadership our youth need in today's world.

Prayer

Oh God, I pray that You will grant me a good attitude. Help me to realize that I stand tallest when I'm on my knees. May I use my disappointments as Your divine appointments. Protect me from being proud of my humility. Amen.

JOHN BRIDGERS

The Will to Win

> . . . what does the Lord require of you but to do justice, and to love kindness, and to walk humbly with your God? (Micah 6:8, RSV).

OUR BAYLOR UNIVERSITY football team of 1963 had a young man who was probably the slowest end in the Southwest Conference. One summer he spent about six weeks in Japan on a Christian youth crusade. He was also president of our campus F.C.A. group, so he kept busy.

He played split end on our team. Being relatively small, he had to learn to be quick with his fakes and certain with his hands. You know what he did for us one year? He caught fifty-one passes in eleven games! That comes close to breaking the national collegiate record set by Lawrence Elkins in 1963.

After the season James Ingram came into my office one day. "James," I said, "you can be proud of your record this season. You did a tremendous job." And he had. In the fourth quarter of the Blue Bonnet Bowl game we were a touchdown behind. He proceeded to catch two touchdown passes and for the game caught a total of eleven passes for 165 yards.

He said, "Well coach, before the season started, I made up my mind on two things. The first was to look back after the season was over and to know that I had done the very best I possibly could. The second was that I knew our quarterback would be throwing to Lawrence Elkins most of the times, because Elkins is faster and has more ability. But I made up my mind I was going to be open anytime that Elkins was bottled up."

This is the kind of spirit every coach would like to have on his team. Certainly it goes along with the unselfish spirit and the teachings of Christ. He taught that if anyone would be first, he must be last and servant of all. This means a Christian must be willing to put the other ahead of him.

There are many other outstanding players I have had the pleasure of coaching. I'll say one thing about my profession, you receive constant inspiration from these young men. I'm proud of every coach and every player we have at Baylor.

An athlete probably doesn't realize the magnitude of his influence on other aspiring young athletes—even on the entire younger generation. Don Trull is one of these athletes. He is undoubtedly one of the most exceptional football players ever to play in collegiate sports. Every youngster in Texas seemed to know him.

I was in Lubbock, Texas—which is quite a distance from Waco, home of Baylor University—for the Southwest Conference meeting. A little boy came up to me and asked if I was Coach Bridgers. He said, "Well, Coach, I just wanted to meet you because you're Don Trull's coach. About two weeks ago Don came up and spoke at our Father and Son banquet. He's the greatest guy I've ever known! I want to come to Baylor."

Don probably doesn't know this, but he has had a great influence on this boy's life. Here is a youngster whose life was made different by a fellow that had his feet on the ground.

When Don graduated from high school in Oklahoma, they said he wasn't big enough to play in the Big Eight Conference. In 1963 when we played Texas, we went into the game undefeated in the conference. Texas was also undefeated. The game was nip and tuck and a real battle all the way. In the early stages of the game Don was running the ball to get a first down and when tackled hard, cut his lip badly. He was bleeding profusely and came out for a while. We tried to patch it up, and at half time we put four stitches in his mouth. With your lips swollen and bleeding it's very difficult to run a team and call signals. Texas finally scored in the third quarter, and in the late stages of the game we took the ball on our thirteen-yard line with about a minute and a half to go. In less than a minute we were down on the Texas nineteen with just twenty seconds to go. Don threw a pass to Elkins which looked like a sure touchdown, but the Texas defensive quarterback came out of nowhere to pick the ball out of Elkins' hands in the end zone and the game was over.

Don walked across the field to congratulate the various Texas players even though the wind was blowing about fifteen to twenty miles per hour and it was raining hard. When the sports writers came into the dressing room and asked questions about the game, Don didn't say a thing, as far as I know, to throw discredit on the game of football or on his opponents who had beaten him that day.

This is the attitude we must have as athletes, to meet triumph and disaster just the same, with poise and integrity.

Being physically fit goes hand-in-hand with spiritual fitness. In 1964 I had a great thrill. I was in Fort Worth with a number of coaches, playing golf with Ben Hogan and his brother. Ben Hogan has always been one of the most inspiring examples I know of in sports. After being crippled in an auto accident, and after being told he would never walk again, he came back and won every major golf championship. And he weighs only 140 pounds!

When we finished our round of golf, he told us this: "When it got down to the crucial point in competition you know what gave me an edge? It was work, hard work.

I always felt if I just worked a little harder than the other fellow, I would have that competitive edge. I felt I could make the shot I needed most." Of course, this is nothing new. But it's encouraging to hear it from this champion.

If you're spiritually fit, you'll always be a winner. Every scoreboard and each contest may go against you, but you're still going to be a winner. The Apostle Paul was a winner. He knew he was a winner; no one could whip him. Even when he was in prison in chains and his life threatened, he didn't sit around in self-pity. You know what he did? He sat down and wrote a letter to his young friend Timothy, trying in every way to encourage Timothy to hold fast to his spiritual life. He said: "I am already on the point of being sacrificed; the time of my departure has come. I have fought the good fight, I have finished the race, I have kept the faith. Henceforth there is laid up for me the crown of righteousness, which the Lord the righteous judge, will award to me on that Day, and not only to me but also to all who have loved his appearing."

This is the faith that makes a winner.

Prayer

Gracious God, inspire me to put the concern of others on the team before my own. Help me to be faithful to my charge as an athlete in setting the best example. I can't do it alone; I need You. Amen.

JIM KAAT

Believing in Christ

> And without faith it is impossible to please him. For whoever would draw near to God must believe that he exists and that he rewards those who seek him (Hebrews 11:6, RSV).

I NEVER HAVE considered myself the "kid who was born with the silver spoon in his mouth," but I have been a rather fortunate person.

Being raised in the little town of Zeeland, Michigan, which houses no theaters or saloons, I found it very easy to go to church, as did 99½ percent of the rest of the population of Zeeland. By a process of elimination, going to church was really the only thing one could do there on Sunday. As I progressed through my early years, I attended church twice each Sunday and sang in all the church pageants and programs that came along. Please bear this in mind, I didn't do these as a youngster because I wanted to, but because my parents felt it was what I should do. As far as I was concerned, Bible verses and praying was for little girls and sissies.

Christianity, or what I considered "goin' to church," was somewhat of a ritual, or habit I had developed. Don't get me wrong, it's a good habit to develop, but at that point in life church to me was like a football game described by a close friend of mine: "A place which many attend, but few understand."

When I reached high school, quite a few of the kids my

age were joining the church or making confession of their faith in Christ. Being a "joiner," I followed suit and took John 3:16 as it is written: "For God so loved the world that he gave his only Son, that whoever believes in him should not perish but have eternal life." I was then age fourteen.

I guess I was a typical teenager. I thought I was grow-up and that I had better start taking things a little more seriously. Becoming a church member was one way I could show the world that I was maturing. During the re-mainder of my high school career my life changed very little. I knew that by attending Church and actually be-coming a church member, I was walking in the right direc-tion. Yet the true meaning of being a Christian and a member of the church was still hazy, and I showed some uncertainty in my steps.

But as I look back, I realize now why my parents were so interested in my taking part in church activities, and why the city of Zeeland put so much emphasis on its being a clean, wholesome place in which to live. I think just about everything we do in life, be it good or bad, shows what kind of upbringing we have had, by both parents and community. I thank my parents and my hometown for showing me the right way.

When I signed my first professional contract in 1957 and started my climb up the ladder to the major leagues, I be-gan to realize the meaning of all the early training I had received. I believe that I was given the ability to play baseball for a reason. Each person has been given the ability to do something in life that can be used to tell others what Christ has meant to him and what the Chris-tian life can mean to others.

If we fail to make the best of that ability, then we have failed God. We have an obligation to God and our fami-lies to dedicate ourselves to do our best in our chosen field of endeavor. In I Corinthians 9:24-27 it's put this

91

way: ". . . in a race all the runners compete, but only one receives the prize? So run that you may obtain it." To win one must deny himself many things that might keep him from doing his best. As athletes we must keep our bodies and minds in top condition or we will not be able to win the prize. The prize we are after as baseball players is naturally the league pennant, which our Minnesota Twins team was able to win in 1965. But the *real* prize we are after as Christians is life eternal which will never disappear as worldly prizes will.

Today I realize that Christianity is not just for children and elderly ladies, but it is also for men. Jesus was a strong man. He preached and taught the Father's Word to all peoples. I firmly believe it is our duty as laymen to let our light shine every day of our lives and attempt to lead others to know Christ personally, as we know Him.

Prayer

Thank you, God for parents and family, who make a Christian home possible. Help me to have a better attitude towards those close to me and to do everything possible to make my home more Christ-like. Amen.

JAMES JEFFREY

Faith

> And whatever you ask in prayer, you will receive, if you have faith (Matthew 21:22, RSV).

FAITH IS as basic in being an athlete, as it is in being a Christian. We need to believe and trust in what the coach tells us, then test the truth of his teachings through practice and playing the game. This kind of trust and belief operates in the Christian life as well.

What is even greater about the Christian life is that anyone can appropriate the truths of the Bible for his own heart through faith. Regardless of the position you play or the team you may be on, the truths of God are for you —for every person. They're not reserved for just those who are successful, for those who have experienced some dramatic kind of answer to prayer, just those who are able to teach a Sunday school lesson, or those who can read from the Bible without making mistakes. Our loving God has something for you, right where you are, in *your* circumstances, with *your* background, with all of *your* mistakes, with all of the anxieties and all of the complexes in you.

The foundation of our faith is that God loves you. He wants you to live in constant fellowship with Him. This love reaches out to everyone—those who have finished college, those who are in professional athletics, or those in the coaching profession—to everyone. But we must believe that He loves us. The best way to know this is to believe in Jesus Christ.

93

Believing in Jesus is very simple, no tricks. According to the Word of God, to believe in Him is to believe that He died for your sins, that God raised Jesus from the dead and that the Master lives today. It also means to put your confidence in Christ's power to forgive sins, to give life, to let you know and enjoy the abundant life, to save you from wanton fears, killing anxieties, undue frustrations, and all the inner conflicts which tear you apart. He wants to help you if you will trust Him.

The only way I can trust someone is to love him. That person needs to know that I love him, too. How wonderful it is to be loved, to have someone honestly care about you.

Bill Carroway played football at Georgetown University for four years while the great Lou Little was coach. Although Bill played on the squad, he hadn't made the first team, and this was the last game of the season, therefore the last football game of his career, his last chance to play.

Because he wanted so to play, he went to the coach's house the night before the game. He knocked on the door and he said, "Coach, I've seen great teams go out on that field in my four years here, but I haven't had a chance to play. I was wondering if you'd give me this opportunity tomorrow, whether it be for one minute, or even one play —just let me get in the game."

The coach said, "I can't promise anything; this game means too much for too many people, but because of the way you've worked for me during the past four years, I'll do the best I can."

Game time came. The stadium was packed; even the bleachers were filled. Two great teams took the field and began to fight—back and forth, up and down the field. At half-time Georgetown University was three points behind. In the second half Lou Little called on all the strategy and football knowledge he had ever known, but nothing would work. His special offense just wouldn't click. Since time was running out, Bill Carroway realized that he might not get in the game, so he put his helmet under his arm and began to walk up and down the sidelines in front of the coach, hoping he would be seen.

The coach did see him, and this must have been his thinking: "I can't gain a thing in the world by sending this inexperienced kid into the game, but what can I lose? What can I lose? I want to reward this boy for the hard way he has worked for me through the years." So he sent Bill Carroway into the game as halfback. On the very first play he took the hand-off from the quarterback, went through the hole in the line, and forty yards down the field before he was pulled down. The people in the stands were standing and cheering. They quickly looked at their programs—his name wasn't even on it! Could it be that this unknown player might save the day?

Every play had to be a pass because of the time remaining. On the next play the quarterback took the snap from the center, faded back into the pocket prepared for him by the linemen, and looked down field. It seemed as if in that split second Bill Carroway had a step on his defender, so the quarterback let loose with a beautiful spiral pass. Bill leaped high into the air and caught it, falling into the end-zone for the winning touchdown. And so the story goes that Georgetown won the championship.

But that's not the important thing—not at all! For as soon as Lou Little had been put down from the shoulders of admiring fans, he went to Bill Carroway's locker, where the little halfback was taking off his uniform. He said, "Bill, in all my many years of coaching I've never seen a boy more determined to succeed than you were today. Nor in my many years of coaching have I seen a boy who did succeed more gloriously than you did today. Tell me, Bill, what was it that made you give one-hundred percent of all you possess to win that game?"

The little halfback looked up into the eyes of the great coach as unashamed as could be and said, "Coach, when I was born, my mother died and all through the years my wonderful father has wanted me to do two things. The first thing was to go to college and get an education. I've done that. Many times the guys would come to my door and say, 'Come on, Bill, let's go out and have a good time; let's go have a blast,' but I said no and stayed in my room, finishing up the assignments so that I might please my dad. I'm going to graduate in a matter of months with honors.

"The second thing my dad wanted me to do, coach, was to play football. You see, I knew my dad would never see me play football because he was blind. Several days ago my dad died and I knew that today would be the first and the last time he would ever have a chance to see me play. So you see, coach, I had to succeed; there were no two ways about it for Bill Carroway; there was just one path."

He knew that the one who loved him was watching him and expecting the greatest from him, and he refused to disappoint that love.

Prayer

Most gracious kind Father, with seriousness of heart and mind I ask You to give me the courage and the faith to believe in You. I pray for all those who are striving to find something better in life that they may come to know of You, keep their eyes upon You and grow spiritually. Grant each of us the courage and the faith not to expect to be spiritual giants over night or even in a week but to hold steadfast to our faith and trust in You. Help us to know and enjoy the abundant life and be faithful to our church and to You. Amen.

III

"CONQUERING"

Life's Common Upsets

PRENTICE GAUTT

Frustrations

> . . . We have peace with God through our Lord Jesus
> Christ. Through him . . . we rejoice in our sufferings,
> knowing that suffering produces endurance, and endur-
> ance produces character, and character produces hope,
> and hope does not disappoint us, because God's love has
> been poured into our hearts through the Holy Spirit which
> has been given to us (Romans 5:1-5, RSV).

IT HAPPENED in our opening game against the Dallas Cow-
boys in 1963. I went out for a short swing pass and just
as I caught the ball, their linebacker hit me in the back
with a hard tackle. I felt a sharp pain, but I got up and
ran one more play before coming out. Our team physician
came over and after checking me said: "Let's take him
and get a blood count; we will have him back in time
to leave with the team tonight." I didn't get out of Dallas
that night; as a matter-of-fact, I spent about three weeks
in Dallas in Baylor Hospital, wondering if they were
going to have to remove my kidney. I prayed because I
was in a tight spot and needed help.

The physican in charge was a Dr. Hurt. He came in and
said: "Prent, everybody else wants to operate, but I believe I am going to take a week, maybe two weeks before
giving you another examination to see if this kidney is as
bad as we think it is. Right now it looks like somebody
took razorblades and just went down the bottom of about
three-quarters of it; only the top part of it is functioning."
Well, this really shook me up. I went back to praying

selfishly. I went through an ordeal which was very exasperating. My wife was still by my side. I could appreciate that, but yet I still didn't feel I was getting the point over to God that this was something I didn't want; something I just didn't want.

Two weeks passed, another X-ray was taken and my doctors found that a little bit more of the kidney had come into function. In three weeks I had five blood transfusions and lost twenty-five pounds. I was completely bed-ridden, but just before the three weeks ended, I had stopped bleeding internally. The doctors decided that if the trend continued, I could be shipped to St. Louis for closer medical supervision. My condition improved so that I was shipped to a St. Louis hospital.

My new doctor's name was Sunshine. I seemed to take on a feeling of hope. He told me that an exploratory operation might be necessary in another week. I prayed even harder than ever. Throughout this week and on the eve of the operation I was terribly lonely. I tried to call home in Oklahoma City, but I couldn't reach anybody. I tried to talk to somebody around the hospital and no one seemed available. I tried watching TV, but nothing satisfied me. I turned off the light and there in the dark I tried to find adequate words to say to God. I wasn't able to find the right words and finally I said: "God, I open my heart to You please come in and take my life, mold it the way that You want. Let me be able to get away from all petty and foolish things that I have desired and have done in the past. I need You and will trust in You completely."

Somehow I was able to go to sleep. Early the next morning they wheeled me to the operating floor, where the surgeon, Doctor Cardonia, was waiting. He said, "Prent, there is one way that we can get away from this operation; we can take you into the Cystoscopy Room. It is kind of painful, but I think that you would prefer

99

this to an operation and maybe we can see something better to do."

They placed me in the room and took a ten-second and a twenty-second shot, then left me. This time I didn't feel alone. There was somebody with me, and as I think back to that time, I can see myself there on that table saying and believing that my kidney was going to be saved. Shortly the doctor returned and said: "Prentice, we can't tell very much from this shot. If we can't tell anything from the other, an operation is necessary."

This may seem strange, but for the first time I was praying not selfishly, but asking what could I do for the Lord. I was completely at peace within. Soon the doctor returned with the biggest grin on his face and he said: "Prent, we've made it. This kidney can be saved: all we need is a little rest." What a great feeling! I knew the Lord had answered my prayer, and I kept wondering why.

They say a man's not supposed to cry, but at this time I shed some tears, because I know that if you are a child of God no matter what you have done, no matter who you are, no matter what color your skin, He will take care of you as He has me.

Prayer

Loving Father, send me not through the paths of ease and comfort, but through the stress and strain of difficulties and disappointments. I know that it is through the fire of ordeal that my spirit is tempered and my mind strengthened to become more aware of Your power and presence. Amen.

DOUG WEAVER

Disappointments

> I know your tribulation and your poverty. . . . Do not fear what you are about to suffer. . . . Be faithful unto death, and I will give you the crown of life (Revelation 2:9-10, RSV).

BEING A CHRISTIAN isn't easy. It is something we attain by constant effort. Athletes and coaches like myself have to get in the fight and battle for what's right. We have to slug it out in our profession; you have to fight it in the parked cars, in the fraternities, in the locker room, at home in the alley. You've got to fight for Christ where it is tough. This takes courage and then some.

My story would be more dramatic if I could say that I was raised out of the gutter. But that's not true. I was brought up in a great Christian home and I knew Christ at an early age. One thing I didn't have at first was courage. I thought what a man believed was his own private business, and I didn't want to talk to him about it. But men I have come to know through the Fellowship of Christian Athletes have given me terrific strength and courage. These are not just ministers, but coaches who are struggling and fighting it out just like me. There is a great strength in witnessing to your faith. There are football players all over this country in every conference who are ready to pull on their pads and really get with it. There are men just like you who are fighting this thing and struggling with it and who are going to make the grade because they persevere in their faith—they stick with it. Oh, I wish I could have all those guys that want to talk about Christians being sissies, and how Christianity is for the birds. These are the guys who think they are tough. I would like to stick them up between four blocking dummies and give them the meat-grinder drill, then the nut-cracker, and then for dessert a real eye-opener. Every ten minutes pow, pow, pow—I would stick them right in there with all the equipment and see how tough they really are. These Christian ball players will hit you and show you no quarter; they'll bust you right out of your lethargy; they will try to beat you out of your position. Then when it's all over, they will see you in the locker room and will tell you that Jesus is Christ. I know these guys; they taught me something, especially in 1960.

There was a fine young athlete from Belville, Kansas, whom I tried to recruit. He had some problems. He was only five feet, eight inches and 160 pounds, a very fine high hurdler, a very fine all-around athlete, but relatively small for college football. His name was Ralph McFillen. I wanted him on my ball club, but he said that he was too small to play Big Eight. I said, "Why?" He told me that all the other coaches he had talked with said he was too small to play in the Big Eight. Well, I'm no saint, but this boy was a hitter. I watcher films of his games and as a 160-pound middle linebacker he was really giving those blockers and ball carriers a rough time. I liked him because he liked to play football, was a good student, had some ambition, and because he thought a great deal of Kansas State University.

Well, he enrolled and played safety man as a regular and half back for two years, at five feet, eight inches, 160 lbs., and then went on to be an All-Conference Big Eight end. You know what I like about Ralph? He did something for me. He knew about the Fellowship of Christian

Athletes before I did. He had been going to their conferences for a couple years and was completely sold on them. He wanted others to know about it. I can see his little notices now on the board: "There will be an F.C.A. meeting at 4:30 tonight," signed "Ralph McFillen." That was in 1960 and 1961.

You know what else I remember? I can see "Ralph" scratched out and "Deacon" written in. It figures doesn't it? Some smart guy. Then I can see "Amen, Brother" written after it. I can see these signs and I figure some fellows are trying to break this guy. I was with him, but I didn't know how to help him. I quickly learned this man didn't need help. You know why they still called him "Deacon" in his senior year? Because now there were about forty other players just like him on our ball club, and they had just elected him the "most inspirational player."

Don't get me wrong. There's no guarantee for popularity or acceptance. You can be all-conference, but do you have the spirit and the fight to slug it out? When you do, others will follow you.

I want to feel the toughness in you. That's important.

A favorite passage of mine is Revelation 2:10. It's terrific. It says ". . . Be thou faithful unto death, and I will give you the crown of life." I like that passage, because it doesn't say "successful." It doesn't say "Be thou successful and I will give you the crown of life." It says, "Be thou faithful." It's no guarantee. Man, I feel that I'm the luckiest guy with legs, as we say in our profession. I've had a few funny things happen. I've had great things happen. I've had an all-losing season. I've had situations where I wondered if I could keep coaching or not, and all this time I was a Christian, believing in Christ as my Saviour. There's no guarantee you are going to be a winner. But believe me, there is a guarantee that you can handle anything, if you get down there and hammer it out for Christ.

You can handle anything not because you deserve it, but because God loves you and gives you His grace. All things are possible through the amazing grace of God.

Prayer

O God, I know that my enthusiasm as a Christian is sustained by my faith. I want my faith to be strengthened rather than weakened by my attitude and conduct. So please be a constant reminder of my dependence upon You so that my trust in You might be more complete. Thank You for the faith that overcomes all difficulties. In the joy of the Master. Amen.

BILL BRADLEY

Sin

> And he called to him the multitude with his disciples, and said to them, "If any man would come after me, let him deny himself and take up his cross and follow me. For whoever would save his life will lose it; and whoever loses his life for my sake and the gospel's will save it" (Mark 8:34-35, RSV).

THE CLOSING CEREMONY of the 1964 Olympics in Tokyo was for me one of the most meaningful moments of the entire Olympic games. There were athletes from all the nations of the world, but unlike the opening ceremony, where we all had entered by country, everyone just walked in a group—a mass of brotherhood—with friends we had made in the Olympic Village. I walked along the way lined with Japanese Boy Scouts; to my left were some of the Italian basketball players that I'd come to know; in front of me was a fellow from Pakistan; to my left were Irishmen in green blazers, and all around were people from all the nations of the world. We filed into the Olympic stadium and assembled on the infield grass.

The lights in the stadium dimmed and as we watched the Olympic torch flicker and finally fade away, everyone on the field joined in the singing of *Auld Lang Syne,* while at the same time five hundred Japanese youths lit torches and waved them in the air.

This was a very emotional experience for me and as I stood there I thought: "Why can't the world be like this? Why can't everybody get along every day like we did these three weeks in the Olympic Village?" Oh, there were "incidents" of a few who didn't get along, but on the whole it was an ideal community. And I asked myself, "Why can't the world be this way?"

During the next few weeks I thought of several reasons. One is that half the world is now Communist. These people are atheists and pride themselves on being that. During the school year five members of the touring Russian team visited the Princeton campus and I had the privilege of showing them around. When we walked into the chapel, one of the younger members, who was about twenty-two, said, "Oh, when do you come here? Right before exams, I bet?" Then added: "We don't need those in Russia." This kind of struck me. Here was a system, an ideology, which was supposedly designed to save the world, but one which actually amounted to plain dictatorship. This is a preventive in the materializing of the Olympic ideal.

Second, there is a crass materialism all around us. There are people who will do anything for a dollar. There are men who would like to have fame and fortune and forget about the man next to them, or the little man down the line.

Then there is hypocrisy. Perhaps hypocrisy exists because so many people say, "Oh, I want the world to be different," but they don't want to be different themselves. It may be that too many of us are thinking just of ourselves.

Well, it may be one of these three things, but a fourth reason has become very clear to me. It's bigger than these other three. The reason that the Olympic ideal can never materialize is that man himself is sinful. I am convinced that the only corrective to this state is Jesus Christ. I believe this absolutely. Jesus Christ and His way of life are the only answer to the creation of a world of true brotherhood and peace.

As I think about these Olympic experiences and the spirit of companionship we enjoyed, I recall another memorable incident. One evening just before competition was to begin, another American and I attended a banquet. Athletes were there from all over the world with only one thing in common: they were Christians. We heard several men speak, one of whom was Rafer Johnson, perhaps the most highly respected athlete in the world. He told the group that it is important to have a physical body and a strong team; it's important to be nimbly alert; but the most important aspect of life is spiritual existence. This statement struck every person in the room.

Later that evening two Americans, two Nigerians, and two New Zealanders were taken to a downtown Tokyo theater and ushered onto the stage. Standing before 1200 Japanese youths dressed in their black student uniforms, these men told these young people of Japan what it meant to them to be Christian.

When I heard the handsome champion from Nigeria give his witness, I thought, "Isn't it true? It's a world-wide brotherhood; it's a world-wide fellowship. It's answering similar questions there as it is here in America, Japan, and everywhere." This Nigerian said the thing that was hardest for him to overcome in becoming a Christian was the way the other fellows in his village made fun of him. Another athlete from the group said his family didn't understand him; there were pressures from all sides to be like everyone in his village. But he cast these all aside and accepted eternity and Jesus Christ.

If Christianity means this, why aren't there more Christians? As I ask myself this question, I come up with many answers. The most obvious is that few of us really have come to know the Master, to understand His way of living, and to practice it daily. The most common questions we need to ask ourselves are: "What does being a Christian mean to me and what is there to becoming a Christian?"

It was difficult for me to say that Jesus Christ was the answer in my life. I was like the average student. I was active in a lot of things in high school, played in sports, kind of passed Christianity aside. Because of what many Christian coaches and other leaders had said at an F.C.A. national conference about being a Christian, I spent many days and nights thinking. I ended up in my freshman year at Princeton University still thinking. I came out of an oral French examination one day, perplexed. I hadn't understood a word the professor had said. I went up to my room and didn't know what to do. I thought, "Well, I'll read the Bible—but where am I going to turn?" I thought, "Well, I'll call home—but that's 1200 miles away. Well, I'll talk to a few friends"—but there weren't any close friends to talk to.

Then I remembered that about two days before I'd received a record from the Fellowship of Christian Athletes conference of the previous summer. I got that record out, went upstairs and borrowed a record player, lay on the floor, and listened to it. As the platter began to spin, and the messages, laughter, and singing began to pour out, I heard some words that I'd have to say changed my life. These were the words of Bob Pettit, a man I'd always admired as much for his religious life as for his basketball career. He said, "We're not playing for the state championship, or for the national championship—we're playing for one thing—and that's the victory of Christ in the hearts of men."

That caught me. Here I was at the end of my first semester, worried about basketball, worried about myself, worried about grades; I had crowded out Jesus Christ. At that point I decided that after two years of questioning, investigating, praying, this was what I wanted. I asked Jesus Christ to come into my life. And I have to say happily, since that time things haven't been quite the same.

Talk about a challenge, or having an exciting life— that's Christianity. I'm tired of some of the things I see. I wish more men would take a stand and speak up for their faith in Christ. It's hard for me, too. I try in a very poor way. But it's a wonderful experience, one that can change your life; it changed mine.

Accepting Christ could be the most important decision that you've ever made in your life, because with Jesus Christ by your side you're a member of a world-wide brotherhood. In Him you have someone who loves you more than anybody in the world. And you know, you and I could possibly change the world if enough of us believe.

Prayer

Most gracious Heavenly Father, give me the courage and will to find your path and follow it one hundred percent. Make me aware that Your Son Jesus Christ died on the cross for my sins and that all I have to do is to accept Him for my life to change; for my life to become full and meaningful, for my life to count. Make me realize that only in my own humble and almost ineffective way can Christianity become real. Make me know that I'm only your tool and your vehicle. Give me all the courage again to stand and carry your spirit. In Jesus' name I pray. Amen.

DON SHINNICK

Being in the Minority

> Therefore, since we are surrounded by so great a cloud of witnesses, let us also lay aside every weight, and sin which clings so closely, and let us run with perseverance the race that is set before us, looking to Jesus the pioneer and perfecter of our faith, who for the joy that was set before him endured the cross, despising the shame, and is seated at the right hand of the throne of God.
>
> Consider him who endured from sinners such hostility against himself, so that you may not grow weary or faint-hearted (Hebrews 12:1-3, RSV).

It takes real courage to be in the minority.

Anyone who has been in sports knows this to be true. Very few times are you always on top. Usually you find yourself battling as an underdog, whether it's in ping-pong, the hundred-yard dash, or some other sort of game. The Bible tells us some of God's minorities who have won great victories.

Noah was in the minority. One day he started to build a large ark. The people around him said, "Now Noah, what in the world are you building this ark for. I mean you know, you've got more things to do. You've got a family and all; what's the idea of the ark?"

Noah replied: "Well I'm preparing for something." Most of the folks laughed and walked away. He was really among the few.

The 1958 championship game between the New York Giants and the Baltimore Colts has been called the greatest football game ever played. We were at Yankee

Stadium playing for the world championship. We were tied after the full sixty minutes, so we went into the first sudden death in professional football history. Now during this crucial period a strange thing happened. The Colts had driven seventy-four yards down to the six-yard line. All we had to do was run three straight running plays right in front of the goal post, and kick the extra point to win. But John Unitas, our quarterback, did a very unusual thing. He threw a diagonal pass out to our right end, who caught it and was tackled on the one. We scored on the next play and won the game. Unitas was in the minority, for most people, including our opponents, expected us to run. But he had prepared for this. On the long march he had tried everything under the moon, but not this particular play. He had the nerve to go with something that the majority never expected. Minority shows itself in so many ways.

Another cause which appeared to be a minority in its beginning, but has become a majority is Christianity. This all came about because one man, Jesus Christ, dared to face His enemies, had the courage to love when others hated, endured torture, pain, and death on the cross just so you and I could know the way of eternal happiness through Him. You think that's not a minority? Try being a Christian when you are in school; try carrying a Bible across campus, see if you're in the minority. Try to get up in front of a group of boys and girls at a social to tell them they shouldn't use dirty language. "You know Christ, He wouldn't like that." Tell them this and see if you'd be in the minority. But thank God, this minority is His majority. I would like to tell you how I had the privilege of being on this team, God's minority. By the grace of God He accepted me into this family we call the Christian team.

For the first eighteen years of my life I thought I was a Christian. I was not only a churchgoer, but always in

111

Sunday school, the youth group, at church picnics, and in anything else these groups had in the daytime. On special holidays I'd salute people coming into church, and salute them going out. I was there morning, noon, and night. So I felt maybe I was a little ahead of the next fellow. So I thought, well, I must be a Christian; I'm doing pretty good along these lines.

Another reason I thought of myself as a Christian is that I knew I wasn't the worst guy in the world, but I wasn't the best either. I was sort of right down the middle. I didn't kick cats. I'd help older ladies across the street, things like this, but that wasn't enough. I thought I was a Christian because I was a doer. If the minister would say, "Let us pray," I'd be the first to pray. I'd say "I believe," and people in front of me would think I was great.

But I suppose the basic reason I thought I was a Christian is that I didn't doubt what my Sunday school teacher had to say about this person Jesus Christ, about the church, the Bible, and all the other doctrines. But my belief was all in my head. It had nothing to do with the heart and soul. It was just like believing in Abraham Lincoln, Plato, and any other historic person.

But twelve years ago somebody finally told me in just a very simple way about this person Jesus Christ. What he told me was that Christ died for the sins of the world. Well, I knew that. But then he brought it a little closer. He said, "Christ died for you, Don Shinnick, and what have *you done* about it? Not your pastor, not your best friend, your mother, or father, but what have you done about it?" After a few of these talks, I realized that I hadn't really put my faith, belief, and trust in this person, Christ.

So one night I went home, got down on my knees and said, "Lord, I want to accept You." I said it in football terms. I said, "Lord I want You as my coach. I want to be on this Christian team. I know I haven't believed the right way, and whatever way is right; please let me believe it." This is when I know I became a Christian. Then and there is where John 1:12 made sense to me: "But to all who received him, who believed in his name, he gave power to become children of God."

I know that being a Christian doesn't stop you from getting a stomach ache. It doesn't stop you from getting clipped from behind. It doesn't stop you from getting hurt in a game. It doesn't stop you from maybe losing a loved one. Five and a half years ago my wife had twins. We lost one of them five days later. Being a Christian doesn't stop all this. But at least now we seek the answers by faith, knowing that God's love sustains us.

There are three things that have helped me in living this Christian life:

1. When we do something wrong, when we aren't living the Christian life, let's confess it. I John 1:19 reads: "If we confess our sins, he is faithful and just, and will forgive our sins . . ." Let's get back on the road with God.

2. Continually ask for God's strength and guidance. When walking down the street, or playing baseball, say, "Lord, I need Your help; give me Your help, give me strength." And He will.

3. Know Christ as best you can. The more we know about Him, the closer we get to Him, the better we know His will for our lives.

I challenge you to be on God's team. In man's sight you may be in the minority; as a Christian in God's sight you're on the winning team. Thank God that His minority becomes victorious.

Prayer

May Your Word and Your life in Jesus Christ be more real to me every day, O God. I need Your help; give me Your strength and wisdom, I ask in His loving spirit. Amen.

BRIAN STERNBERG

Suffering

> But whatever gain I had, I counted as loss for the sake
> of Christ. . . . For his sake I have suffered the loss of all
> things, and count them as refuse, in order that I may gain
> Christ and be found in him, not having a righteousness of
> my own, . . . but that which is through faith in Christ,
> the righteousness from God that depends on faith; that I
> may know him and the power of his resurrection, and may
> share his sufferings, becoming like him in his death, that
> if possible I may attain the resurrection from the dead
> (Philippians 3:7-11, RSV).

I despise being paralyzed as I have been for the past
few years; I don't think I would be normal if I didn't.
But there are many lessons I have learned from this
experience.

For one thing, I found out the hard way that no man
has the absolute answer to your problem. You may talk
to person after person whom you respect, but in the final
analysis your decision for any problem must be between
you and God. No man can give you the final answer satis-
factorily. I know. I have tried this approach. I thought
somewhere there had to be someone who would tell me
bluntly if I was going to be able to beat this thing or not.
My search started with my girl at that time. The fact that
I am a Christian now is due primarily to her.

When I was hurt, I was not a Christian. I had built a
dependence upon all sorts of other things. I knew about
Christianity, but I wasn't a Christian. After a few weeks

of being flat on my back with virtually no movement at all, it became evident to me that I was not going to be able to beat this thing just with determination, gritting my teeth, setting my mind, and saying, "I am going to do this on my own." I tried to believe that I could do it just by trying hard and that's all. It didn't work that way. It took a while, but the thing my girl was saying finally began to sink in. That I had only one direction in which I could travel—that was toward God.

I talked to other respected people, but none of them had a complete answer for me. I learned from them, but no reasonable answer satisfied me. After months of deep soul-searching, conversations with dozens of friends, mental and emotional strain, and physical agony I came to realize and believe that no one ever truly comes to God except through some real suffering.

In my case I was surprised that I didn't go the other way and turn to bitterness; but amazingly enough that wasn't the case. I became a Christian and little did I know that I would be preaching Christ at this point of my life. I certainly wouldn't have believed it if someone had told me at the time of my accident. It seems to me most people go through some struggle in becoming a Christian. There may be a mental change, an emotional upheaval, a social adjustment—many different reachings. One thing I found out is that how well you respond to God is affected by how self-sufficient you were before accepting Him. Before my accident I was completely independent. When I was suddenly laid on my back, every block that supported every pillar seemed to collapse. The only thing left was to build on Christ and I took a long time to learn this.

This is where athletics can help. I have a burning desire to get on my feet again and walk that has never changed. That same determination sustains my desire to know God and to become more Christ-like each day. Without that desire there would be nothing gained.

Another requirement in being a Christian is the willingness to pay the price. Are you really willing to sacrifice in order to continue in the Christian life? I have lost some things very very dear to me in the last year and a half. One pays the price sometime just to exist. I don't say, this to solicit sympathy, but every waking moment is spent in some degree of pain, ranging from that just barely tolerable to that which seems to be unbearable. Sometimes I may be ready to leave for a speaking engagement and find that I can't sit up. But somehow, some way by the help of many prayers and much personal effort sometimes I'm able to make it. There are days, however, when I'm not able to muster the physical strength to get out. When this happens, I believe the Lord is saying that it is better to wait until another day.

I can say that if this accident hadn't happened to me I might not have become a true Christian. My self-sufficiency was at its peak when I held the world's record: it took something powerful and devastating as this to make it possible for me to become a Christian. I believe my faith is firmly planted now so that it will never falter when I stand and walk again. I won't go back to what I was, I know that. When I do get on my feet, I will be standing for the Lord; I will be able to do so much more than I am able to do now.

The odds are about 99.9 to 1 against my type of injury ever happening to anyone else. Yet, something is going to happen to everyone in body, mind, or spirit to some degree in the course of his life. Be ready to pay the price. Be willing to make life's adjustment with the help of other people, but ultimately through your relationship with God through Jesus Christ. If you can make it without having to go through what I did, more power to you.

I wouldn't wish this on anybody, unless it is the only way to bring that person to know Christ.

Prayer

Our precious Heavenly Father, I pray that Your spirit will go with every person who is in special need that he may look to You and find the power to overcome all adverse circumstances. I pray that each person who reads this book will be encouraged by the faithful life and joyful declaration of these many athletes and coaches. Help me to be worthy of the opportunities You have given me to bear witness to your love and power. In Jesus' name. Amen.

FRANK McGUIRE

Adversity

> And he sat down and called the twelve; and he said to them, "If any one would be first, he must be last of all and servant of all." And he took a child, and put him in the midst of them; and taking him in his arms, he said to them, "Whoever receives one such child in my name receives me; and whoever receives me, receives not me but him who sent me" (Mark 9:35-37, RSV).

I HAVE BEEN coaching basketball for twenty-nine years, first at Xavier High in New York City, then St. John's University, the University of North Carolina, a while with the Philadelphia Warriors, and now in my present position at the University of South Carolina. I never have lost sight of the challenge to develop the full man in mind, body, and spirit among players because I was coached that way. My Catholic background instilled this within me in our private schools.

There are five characteristics which I have lived by in coaching and which I intend to live by as long as I do coach: (1) loyalty to your teachers, your coaches, your parents. Not a blind loyalty, but a mutual trust where you honestly share your thoughts and feelings in a climate of trust and respect. You're always a bigger man for this; (2) confidence by practice; (3) self-control—as a coach teaching self-control by your bench manners, by being able to take the decision of an official even though you may not like it; (4) discipline—I can tell how a team is disciplined by their attitude on and off the court; (5)

religion—we encourage every boy to go to the church of his choice. We like the boys to pray together.

Basketball is one part of my life, the other is my family. The challenge of my life came in June 29, 1953, when we had our third child. I have two lovely daughters and two lovely grandsons. One daughter in her twenties lives in North Carolina, and the other in her teens is at home. We also have a little boy fourteen years old, a palsy victim, who is so crippled he does not walk or talk, but he is the greatest part of our lives. He was born on June 29th, 1953. At that time I was still coaching at St. John's. I went up to the hospital at two o'clock in the morning and the doctors told me that there was no hope for the child—my only boy was dying. And, they added, "if he does live, he will be hopelessly crippled." They didn't know what caused it; they had no valid reasons. Since I was of no help there, the doctors suggested I take a walk. I walked the city of New York. What a lonesome city that is sometimes! I was born and raised in the west side of New York. I pride myself on saying I know New York City better than any policeman or fireman alive, because I am one of the natives. But that night there was nothing. It was the biggest and the most lonesome city. As I walked, I thought of all the people who have healthy children and asked, "Why should this happen? How did this happen?"

I didn't know the extent of the damage or the injury. So finally at six o'clock in the morning I walked into a little chapel on Sixteenth Street, where I had gone to school. I sat there and prayed for hours. Finally I went back to the hospital and found that our child would live. My wife was well, so we brought our boy home after a month.

Since that time we have tried every way in this world to get help; every way to try to teach him to walk. Every day it was another challenge to see if he would take a

119

step, to get him to lift his hand, maybe to feed himself. All this time I had been coaching these great athletes at St. John's and at the University of North Carolina, seeing some boys just wasting their lives, thinking how good God has been to them, and all the time just praying and hoping that this boy might someday walk.

In the summer of 1964 we were happily invited to take our son to a rehabilitation center in New York, in West Haverstraw. We experienced a very difficult day after these many years—we had to leave him. As I turned to go, he slid out of the wheel chair and tried to come with me. I just had to run out of the place. During all this we had continuous conversations with the good Lord asking Him to take care of our boy and to grant us wisdom as parents. Every night we visited him. He is doing well and is now back home. The great doctors performed wonders in helping him try to learn how to walk.

I think it was Thursday of the last week when I was leaving the hospital, the last three-week period, I saw boys all over, little fellows, some on sleds. Some had little props to push themselves. Others couldn't turn on their sides, others were without arms. Some couldn't see. All were happy—all were happy and having a wonderful time.

One little boy became very friendly with my boy. They had been in the same room. This sixteen-year-old boy, with no speech whatsoever, maybe weighing fifty some odd pounds, with a brilliant mind, was able to type using one finger. He had a spelling board on his lap. He drove me crazy, because I was never a good speller to begin with. And this boy has some vocabulary. First time I met him, he looked at me and he spelled out: "What's your job?"

And I said, "Coach."

Then he asked: "Pro or college?"

"Boy," I thought, this guy's a ringer; better get out of

here." But I waited and discovered this boy was going home. He was going to leave because his whole ambition was to get a high school diploma and he couldn't get it there. His mother told me this diploma is all he lives for, all he wants. He wrote this little farewell note to the boys before leaving: "This will be the last thing I'll write to you (the group of boys), because I'm going home. Just before I go, I would like to leave a few thoughts with you. We all have setbacks during life, some more than others, but to find a place like this filled with wonderful and devoted men and women willing to give us so much out of their busy lives, you know that God has had His hand out to lead you every step of the way. Oh, yes I know its a hard road to travel, but if we have faith, God will give us the ambition to find that pot of gold at the end of the rainbow. Now I want to thank my PT therapist, who has made my legs straighter (his legs were not straight), my OT therapist, who has helped me with better use of my hands (probably one finger), and my speech teacher, who has worked so faithfully with me (there's not a sound). Then to this wonderful school. They have let me know the joy of helping others who are less fortunate than I. Whatever my problems they have all tried to work them out. Next, I would like to thank the nurses, the aides, and the recreation teachers for the parties, movies, and extra snacks. They never seem to tire of helping us. Now comes the hardest part of my farewell. I must say good-bye to the world's best doctors, who have become such good friends. Whatever I've needed, they've all been there to help. And in saying good-bye I shall pray that God will help you all reach your pot of gold and will continue His many blessings and allow us all to meet again very soon."

It's unbelievable that such boys have these dreams in their hearts—dreams of a high school diploma.

Pick a goal in life, pick something worth going after,

something worth striving for. If it's to be an All-American, try to be the very best. Shoot for the moon, that's one thing. Go for the very highest. And while you're shooting for the moon, while you're going for this goal, remember you have to pay the price. The price might be constant practice, constant heartache, constant devotion and loyalty to your coaches. Give everything you have of your bodies, your minds, and your souls; give all you have. And trust in God's judgment. You can always depend on Him. We have discovered that He will give you the courage to conquer, regardless of the problem.

Prayer

Build me a son, O Lord, who is strong in spirit and in truth. Through my life may my son, my family, my players, and others come to know You and to know that You are the foundation of all knowledge and truth and love. Amen.

BOB RICHARDS

Temptations

> These things I have spoken to you, that my joy may be in you and that your joy may be full.
>
> "This is my commandment, that you love one another as I have loved you. Greater love has no man than this, that a man lay down his life for his friends. You are my friends if you do what I command you (John 15:11-14, rsv).

I'M POSITIVE THAT if Jesus were here today He would use the stories of sports as a means of relating great truths just as He used the story of a father with two sons; five girls going to a wedding; a farmer sowing seeds. The sports world rings with truths because it talks about life and what it takes to be a winner.

As I look at champions in the sports world, I see few as the great athletes. I wish I could tell you that it's the masses who make the championship level. If ever a man was separated from the ordinary, it is in the world of sports. You've got to make up your mind you're not going to be mediocre; you're going to be among the dedicated few.

I went to a small college in Virginia and as a pole-vaulter had won the Mason and Dixon Conference championship at 12′6″. I'm ashamed to mention it. Junior high school kids are jumping this high today! But in my limited circumstances and environment I thought 12′6″ was wonderful. I transferred to the University of Illinois on a track scholarship. The first opportunity I had I swaggered out on that field with my pole in hand to show the boys how to vault. I'll never forget, right in front of my eyes, three men ran down the runway and jumped 14'.

You know, today I could hug them; those men made me. Boy, my ego went out the bottom of my socks. I started lifting weights like I never had before, climbing rope, making sprints—I stayed out there an hour after those guys went home. I had to make 14' to even make that team!

We all have our little goals that we think are great; but they are not. Other people are aiming for the stars; they're going for world records. Get next to them. You'll find out they're the same size and stature as you are—they have the same potential.

It's always the few that uphold the honor of America in the Olympic games. The great masses are content to be indolent and soft. It's always the few people who build churches. It's the few people who are scholars. It's the few people who hold this nation together from the standpoint of statesmanship. I think back in my own limited experience with the Fellowship of Christian Athletes—it was the few dedicated men and their wives who made this organization what it is today. It's always the dedicated few.

Jesus put it this way—"Strive to enter into the straight gate, because it's the wide way that leads to mediocrity." A lot of people go that way. It's a straight gate and it's a narrow way that leads into life. Only a few find it!

You've also got to welcome competition if you're going to be great. You can't escape it. It isn't a question of whether you are going to have it or not—you're in it. Young kids are going to compete for grades, they're going to compete for love, they're going to compete in the economic order, and they're going to compete against the Soviet Union and communism the rest of their lives. We'd better be prepared to compete. I think it's the greatest thing that can happen to us. Pity the man who isn't amongst tough competition.

In the microscope of the sports world, you also see hurt and pain. You know what comes out of the Olympics over and over again? Hurt! Pain! Agony! The great coach at Indiana University, Jim Councilman, put it this way: "I've never seen a world record broken but what the athlete went through hurt, pain, and agony."

I watched Kathy Ferguson in the Olympics, seventeen years of age, biting her lip; she was in this backstroke, struggling against her closest competitor. She was about six inches behind. She could hardly feel her legs. You could just look down almost into the heart of that kid, battling, struggling, nine yards, eight, seven, six—she kept hanging on, she kept digging. She could hardly feel her arms, as they went into the end just barely to win. Afterwards all I could think to ask was: "Kathy, what did you do in the pain?"

This beautiful seventeen-year-old girl grabbed her mother by the arm—she could hardly control her tears— here was such a moment of glory—and she said, "Bob, I just kept praying: 'Please, God, help me keep going; please, dear God, help me keep going.' " Many of these great athletes call on God in pain.

Strange as it may seem, when you go through hurt, you achieve power. Sure it hurts to stretch your lungs, it hurts to stretch those muscles. But when you do it, the next time you have more capacity and more power. You can't be great in sports without pain. There is no scholarship without pain. There is no statesmanship without pain.

John F. Kennedy went through pain just about every moment of his presidential career. And so do many others. Would the Christian movement have been anything without pain? There is no spiritual victory without pain. The biggest illusion in America today is that we can achieve greatness without pain. You must go through this experience before you can achieve it.

On every Olympic stadium there are three Latin words, which translated mean: "Higher, Swifter, Stronger." Every four years these young champions come along competing against each other and breaking every record. They do go higher, they do become stronger, they do run faster.

I think of Brutus Hamilton, who a few years back wrote a book, *The Ultimates of Man,* levels beyond which men could not go. You know who is breaking these ultimates today—junior high and senior high school kids! They thought the human constitution wouldn't take a four-minute mile—it would break in pieces. We have a seventeen-year-old running under four minutes in the mile in Kansas; an eighteen-year-old boy breaking all the long distance records; and a high-school boy jumping 16′ 6″ in the pole vault—he barely missed seventeen feet.

You know what thirteen-year-old girls are doing? Remember Johnny Weismuller, the great Tarzan of the Apes? He held fifty-four American records at one time! He was an Olympic champion. They claimed Johnny Weismuller as the greatest swimmer of all time; no one would ever beat him! Guess who's breaking Johnny Weismuller's world's records today? Thirteen-year-old girls!

I think America needs a dedicated few who will pay the price—people who will compete—people who can think under a pressure-packed hour—people who will hurt, who will go through pain—people who will stretch themselves 'higher, stronger, faster.'

The greatest man who ever lived was a young man. He was all alone. He was among the dedicated few. The world collapsed about Him; He fought thirstily against it; He won the battle. In the pressure of hate—He thought love. In the pressure of lies and propaganda—He thought truth. In the pressure of crime, violence, passion—He thought mercy, forgiveness, justice. He hurt; He stretched the human frame to its highest known concept. He gave Himself because He believed a man could lead a higher life, a man could be stronger, he could run a faster race.

You know what He said about you and me? And this is the real thrust and basis of the Fellowship of Christian Athletes. He said that every man could be like God.

Prayer

Help me to be like Thee, Father, as I know You through Jesus Christ. This is Your will; let it be mine. Amen.

HIEBERT LIBRARY

3 6877 00041 4788

DATE DUE

FEB 25 '71			
DEC 16 '80			
FEB 5 '85			
JA 2 '91			
JE 9 '92			
MY 19'94			

DEMCO 38-297